The Mourning After Sunday:

Grieving While Black

____

By: _Sherri D. Jones_

THE MOURNING AFTER SUNDAY: Grieving While Black
Copyright © 2026 by SHERRI D. JONES

ACKNOWLEDGEMENTS

This book exists because of love.

The love of those who have gone on before me, whose presence shaped me in ways I am still discovering. The love of those who walk alongside me now, holding me when I cannot hold myself. The love that spans generations, that bridges the space between grief and healing, that reminds me I am never truly alone.

To those who have gone on before me.

Mom and Dad.
Lynda Joyce Jones and Claud Austin Jones III.

You are woven into every page of this book. Your lives. Your love. Your loss. The way you shaped me. The way losing you broke me open. The way your absence taught me things your presence never could. I carry you with me in ways that words cannot fully capture, but I have tried. This book is my testimony that love does not end with death, that grief is the price we pay for connection, and that you live on in the work I do, the words I write, and the healing I pursue.

Spiritual Mother.
Yvonne Peterson.

The spiritual mother God graced me with. You saw me when I could not see myself. You spoke life when I was drowning in death. You reminded me that even in grief, there is still movement, still beauty, still the possibility of joy. When God sent you to me, I did not yet know how desperately I needed a mother's wisdom, a mother's love, a mother's unwavering belief that I would survive this. You told me to keep dancing, and in doing so, you gave me permission to live fully even while grieving deeply. This book would not exist without your encouragement, your prayers, and your presence in my life when I needed it most.

To my tribe who is still here, walking alongside me.

My Provision.
Terri Jones-Salter and De'Andre Salter.

Sister. Brother (in law). The ones who heard me say "I need help" and did not hesitate. The ones who showed up when I was sinking. The ones who have walked every step of this grief journey with me, never rushing me, never abandoning me, never making me feel like my pain was too much. You are my provision in the truest sense. The people God placed in my life to ensure I would not have to carry this alone. Your love has been constant, your support unwavering, your belief in me unshakeable even when I could not believe in myself. This book is only possible because you held space for my healing long before I knew how to hold it for myself.

My Family.
The Salter Family

You opened your hearts and your homes. You did not see me as someone marrying into the family but as family, fully and completely. Your love has been a gift I did not know I needed until I had it. Thank you for making room for me, for my grief, for all of who I am.

My Community.
Impact Church Worldwide.

You became the community that held me when I was falling apart. When I walked through your doors carrying more pain than I knew how to name, you did not turn away. You did not require me to have it all together. You did not expect me to grieve quietly or quickly. You made space for my whole self, broken pieces and all, and you loved me through the darkest times.

In you, I found aunts who checked on me and prayed over me. Uncles who offered wisdom and protection. Cousins who walked alongside me in their own journeys and made me feel less alone in mine. Prayer warriors who interceded when I could not find words to pray for myself. Friends who became family, who showed up consistently, who reminded me that I was not abandoned even when loss had taken so much.

You taught me that church is not just a building or a Sunday service. It is a people. A community that bears one another's burdens. A family that stays when things get hard. A place where brokenness is not hidden but held, where grief is not rushed but witnessed, where healing happens not in isolation but in connection.

This is what church should be. A refuge. A home. A place where the wounded can come and be tended to without shame. Where strength is not the only acceptable presentation. Where vulnerability is met with compassion rather than judgment. Where people are loved not for what they can contribute but simply because they belong.

You showed me this kind of church. You embodied it. You lived it out in ways that changed me, that healed me, that gave me hope not just for my own recovery but for what community can be when it is rooted in genuine love.

I am forever grateful that I get to call Impact Church Worldwide my home, my family, my community. You raised me in ways that go beyond Sunday mornings. You shaped my understanding of what it means to belong, to be held, to be loved through the hardest seasons of life.

My Catalyst.
Nicole Alston.

When my grief story started, you were there. You remembered my mom in ways that are unimaginable and continue to keep her legacy alive. Your faithfulness to God's voice has been a gift to my healing, a reminder that I am seen, known, and cared for not just by the people around me but by a God who speaks through them. You are a keeper of my mother's memory and a witness to my grief. Both matter more than I can express.

My Answered Prayer.

Dr. G.

To the therapist who slowed down enough to go back to 1999 with me, who sat with thirteen-year-old me and let her finally grieve. Your patience, your presence, your willingness to trust the process even when it was slow and difficult, made healing possible.

————

To God, who has held me through every loss, every tear, every moment when I thought I could not continue. Who gave me this calling, this purpose, this work. Who continues to walk with me, to guide me, to remind me that even in the valley of the shadow of death, I am not alone.

To my professors, mentors, and colleagues in the field of social work who encouraged this work, who affirmed that Black grief matters, who support my calling even as it is still forming, still searching, still trying to find its voice.

To the ancestors whose names I do not know but whose strength I carry. Whose grief was never acknowledged but whose survival made my life possible. This book is part of the healing you deserved but did not receive. I carry your story forward.

And to you, the reader, who picked up this book. Who is brave enough to look at grief honestly. Who is willing to do the hard work of healing. Who deserves to be seen, to be heard, to be held in your pain. Thank you for trusting me with this journey. May you find in these pages the permission, the validation, the hope you need.

This book is all of ours.

The grief that shaped it. The love that sustained it. The hope that it might make the path a little less lonely for someone else walking this road.

We are worth the healing. And we do not have to do it alone.

TABLE OF CONTENTS

Chapter 1:

The Loss That Changed My Life

Grief did not enter my life quietly.

It arrived suddenly, deeply, and without permission, and it changed the way I see everything.

Before loss, I believed in strength as endurance. I believed in faith as certainty. I believed that if you kept moving, kept praying, kept showing up, the pain would eventually stay behind you. I thought grief was something that happened to other people, in other families, in stories I heard whispered after church services or at family reunions. I believed that if you loved God enough, if you served faithfully enough, if you honored your parents and walked uprightly, somehow you would be spared from the deepest kinds of sorrow. I did not yet understand that grief is not something you "get over." It is something you learn to carry.

My grief came through the loss of someone who shaped my world.

The year was 1999. The day was Sunday. I can still see my dad's face when the phone rang that morning, the way his expression shifted from annoyed from the early morning call to concerned in the space of a single breath.

The doctors were calling to tell him that my mother who had been in the hospital for a while at this point was having trouble breathing and panicking. I watched him move through our living room with an urgency I had never seen before, grabbing his keys, his hands shaking slightly as he bent down to tie his shoes. His movements were rushed but mechanical, like his body knew what to do even while his mind struggled to catch up to what was happening.

"I'll be right back," he said, his voice steady but his eyes betraying something else. Fear, maybe. Or the kind of knowing that sits in your chest before your mind catches up.

I nodded, still in my pajamas, still believing that "right back" meant what it always meant. Still believing that whatever was happening at the hospital would be fixed, managed, handled. That my father would drive there, talk to the doctors, hold my mother's hand, and everything would settle back into its proper place like it had done time and time again. That we would still make it to church, maybe just a little late. That life would continue as it had always continued.

But when he returned, everything had changed.

The person whose presence anchored my sense of safety, love, and identity was gone. My mom was gone.

I remember the way he stood in the doorway of my bedroom, not quite stepping inside, as if crossing the threshold would make it real. His shoulders were slumped in a way I had never seen. His eyes were red but dry, like he had already cried all he could cry in the car on the way home, and now there was nothing left but this awful emptiness. I remember the sound of his voice, hollow and distant, as he spoke words I could not fully comprehend.

"She's gone," he said. Just those two words. Simple. Final. Devastating.

I remember thinking that if I stayed very still, if I did not move or breathe too loudly, maybe time would reverse itself. Maybe she would walk through the door, laughing at how worried we had been, telling us she was fine, she was always fine. She had a way of making everything seem manageable, of turning worry into worship, of reminding us that God was in control even when life felt chaotic.

But she did not walk through that door.

When she died, it felt as though the ground beneath me shifted. Life did not simply continue; it broke into tiny pieces like a glass jar shattering against a hardwood floor. The thirteen-year-old version of myself who existed before that moment no longer fit inside the life that followed. That girl, the one who knew her mother's voice, her scent, the way she prayed out loud, the sound of her heels clicking down the hallway, she vanished the moment those words left my father's mouth.

I sat there on the edge of the bed, still in my pajamas, trying to make sense of what had just happened. My mind could not hold it. Could not process it. It kept sliding away from the truth, searching for some other explanation, some way to rewind the morning and start again.

But there was no rewinding. There was only forward, into a life I did not know how to navigate without her.

And yet, the world expected me to keep going.

In many Black families, grief is not something we sit with, it is something we survive. We are taught to be strong, to pray harder, to push forward. Crying is private. Vulnerability is limited. Pain is endured quietly, behind closed doors, in the shower where no one can hear you, late at night when everyone else is asleep. We learn early that our grief cannot be too loud, too visible, too disruptive. That we must hold it together for the sake of those around us, for the children who are watching, for the family members who need us to be strong, for the church community that expects us to testify about God's faithfulness even in our darkest moments.

I did what I had been taught to do.

That Sunday morning, after the stream of house visitors left from giving their condolences, women carrying pies and Tupperware containers, men gripping my father's shoulder in silent solidarity, voices murmuring "God has a plan" and "She's in a better place," I got dressed for church.

The visitors had started arriving within an hour of my father's return. Word spread quickly in our church community. One phone call became two, became ten, became a steady stream of people at our door. They brought food because that is what you do. They offered prayers because that is what you say. They hugged my father and touched my shoulder and told me I was so brave, so strong, so mature for my age.

I did not feel brave. I felt numb.

I stood in front of my closet later that morning, my hands trembling as I buttoned my dress. The same dress I had worn many

Sundays before, when my mother had been alive to tell me I looked beautiful. The same dress that now felt like a costume for a role I no longer knew how to play. My fingers fumbled with the buttons. Everything felt wrong. The dress felt too tight around my chest, too loose around my shoulders. Nothing fit the way it had just a week ago.

My father knocked softly on my bedroom door. "We should go," he said quietly. "Your mother would want us to go."

I wondered if that was true. I wondered what my mother would actually want, if she could speak to us now. Would she want us sitting in church pews pretending we were okay? Or would she want us to stay home, to let ourselves fall apart, to stop performing strength we did not feel?

But I did not ask these questions out loud. Instead, I finished getting dressed and followed my father to the car.

My father drove us to church in silence. The radio stayed off. The windows stayed up. The world outside continued as if nothing had shattered, as if mothers did not die on Sunday mornings, as if thirteen-year-old girls were expected to sit in church pews and pretend they were not drowning. I watched other families walking into the church building, laughing, chatting, their children running ahead. They looked so normal. So untouched. So whole.

I wanted to scream at them. I wanted to tell them that the world had ended. That nothing made sense anymore. That they should stop acting like everything was fine when my mother was dead.

But I did not scream. I walked quietly beside my father, my hands clasped in front of me, my face carefully composed.

I remember sitting in the back row, feeling like it was all a dream. The sanctuary looked the same, same wooden pews, same faint smell of lemon polish and old Bibles. The pulpit where my mother had preached in countless times stood empty. The choir stand where she had lifted her voice in praise was filled with familiar faces, but her seat remained vacant. Everything felt different. Distorted. Like I was watching my life happen to someone else, like I had been pulled out of my own body and was floating somewhere above it, observing from a distance.

Even after the pastor announced to the congregation that my mom, the minister, the praise dance leader, the armor bearer, the Sunday school teacher, the woman whose voice could fill a room with worship, was gone, I could not make it feel real.

People turned to look at me. I felt their eyes, their pity, their discomfort. Some reached out to touch my hand. Others nodded solemnly. A few cried openly, their grief on display in ways mine could not be. I sat frozen, my hands folded in my lap, my face carefully neutral, my heart screaming inside a body that had learned to be still.

I wondered what they saw when they looked at me. Did they see a grieving daughter? Or did they see what I was trying so hard to show them: a good girl, a strong girl, a girl who trusted God's plan even when that plan made no sense?

The service felt endless. Songs I had sung a hundred times before now felt hollow. Scriptures about God's comfort and peace sounded like empty promises. When it was finally over, when people filed out of their pews and made their way toward me, I braced myself for more condolences, more hugs from people, more well-meaning words that only made the ache worse.

Inside, I was screaming. I did not want my mother to be with Jesus. I wanted her here, with me. I did not care if heaven needed another angel. I needed my mother. And no amount of Scripture or sentiment could fill the gaping hole her absence had left behind.

I thought that was the end of it. I thought that one loss, however devastating, was all I would have to carry.

I was wrong.

When my dad died in 2015, the grief was different. Sharper. More isolating. By then, I knew what loss felt like, but knowing did not make it easier. If anything, it made it worse. Because this time, I knew exactly what was coming, the empty spaces, the phantom phone calls I would want to make, the holidays that would never feel whole again, the questions that would go unanswered, the comfort that would never return.

This time, I knew about the first moments of waking up in the morning when, for just a second, you forget they are gone. The moment when reality crashes back in and you remember all over again. I knew about the way grief changes shape over time, how it can feel manageable one day and utterly crushing the next. I knew about the loneliness of grieving in a world that expects you to move on after a few weeks, a few months, maybe a year at most.

This time, there was no illusion of returning to normal. This time, I was an adult, and adults do not get to fall apart. They do not get to curl up on the floor and refuse to move. They have jobs, responsibilities, bills, people depending on them. They are expected to be functional, productive, put together. To grieve on their own time, in their own space, without disrupting the flow of daily life.

So, I did what I had learned to do. I immediately returned to work. I showed up for others. I answered emails, attended meetings, smiled when expected, nodded at the right moments. I convinced myself that resilience meant not falling apart. That strength meant keeping everything together, no matter how much the seams were straining, no matter how close I was to unraveling completely.

I remember sitting at my desk days after his funeral, staring at my computer screen, trying to focus on a project that suddenly felt completely meaningless. A coworker stopped by to ask how I was doing. "I'm okay," I said automatically. "Just taking it one day at a time."

It was a lie. I was not okay. But saying I was not okay would have required explanation, vulnerability, the kind of emotional exposure that felt impossible in that moment. So, I smiled, thanked her for asking, and turned back to my work.

But inside, I was unraveling.

There were days when my body carried the weight before my mind could name it. Tightness in my chest that made breathing feel like effort. Fatigue that sleep could not fix, the kind that settled into my bones and made even simple tasks feel monumental. Moments when I felt disconnected from myself, from others, from God, like I was floating somewhere above my life, watching it happen but not quite living it.

My body kept score even when my mind tried to pretend everything was fine. I would wake up exhausted after a full night's sleep. My shoulders would ache with tension I could not release. My stomach would knot at random moments throughout the day, responding to a grief my conscious mind was trying to suppress.

I could not explain why simple tasks felt heavy. Why opening my email felt overwhelming. Why phone calls from friends went unanswered. Why joy felt distant, like something happening in another room that I could hear but not access.

People would invite me to dinner, to church events, to girls' nights out, and I would say yes with every intention of going. But when the day arrived, I could not bring myself to leave the house. The thought of putting on clothes, driving across town, making small talk, pretending to be present when I felt so absent from my own life, it all felt like too much.

So, I would cancel at the last minute. Make excuses. "Not feeling well." "Something came up." "Can we reschedule?" Eventually, people stopped inviting me. And I told myself I preferred it that way, even though the loneliness was crushing.

I only knew that something inside me had shifted, and I did not have language for it.

No one taught me how to grieve.

Not in school, not in church, not in the self-help books that promised healing in five easy steps. I did not see myself reflected in books about loss. The faces on the covers were not mine. The stories did not sound like mine. The examples did not include mothers who died suddenly, fathers who followed too soon, communities where strength was survival and vulnerability was weakness.

The grief books I found talked about support groups and therapy and "feeling your feelings." But they did not talk about what it meant to grieve in a culture that views emotional vulnerability as weakness. They did not talk about the pressure to be the strong one, the one who holds the family together, the one who testifies about God's goodness even while your heart is breaking. They did not talk about the shame of admitting you are struggling, the fear that seeking help means you lack faith or strength or resilience.

I did not hear stories that sounded like mine. I did not see research that included people who looked like me, prayed like me, or came from communities like mine. The social workers, therapists, and psychiatrists that would cross my path had nothing in common with me. They meant well, I believe that, but they did not understand. They had frameworks and theories and diagnostic criteria, but they did not have the language for what it meant to grieve while Black, to hold sorrow in a body that history has demanded stay strong, to mourn in a culture that values moving forward over sitting with pain.

When I finally worked up the courage to see a therapist after my father died, she asked me to describe my grief. I told her about the exhaustion, the disconnection, the way I felt like I was watching my life from outside my body. She nodded and made notes and suggested cognitive behavioral techniques. "Try to identify the negative thought patterns," she said. "Challenge them with more positive self-talk."

But my grief was not a negative thought pattern. It was not something I could think my way out of. It was a physical, emotional, spiritual upheaval that touched every part of my existence. And her suggestions, however well-intentioned, felt like they were addressing a completely different problem than the one I was experiencing.

I did not return for many sessions after that.

What I felt did not fit the frameworks I was offered. The stages of grief felt too linear, too neat, too white. The models of healing did not account for generational trauma, for the weight of carrying not just my own loss but the echoes of losses my ancestors never got to mourn. The advice to "express your feelings" did not acknowledge that for many of us, expression was a luxury we could not afford, a vulnerability that felt dangerous in a world that already saw us as too emotional or too angry or too much.

I thought about the enslaved ancestors I never knew, who had their children sold away from them and were expected to keep working the fields the next day. I thought about the generations of Black women who had swallowed their grief and kept moving because survival demanded it. Their stories were not in the grief research. Their experiences were not reflected in the therapeutic models. Their pain was invisible, unacknowledged, unnamed.

And so, I wondered if something was wrong with me.

Maybe I was grieving incorrectly. Maybe I was too sensitive, too weak, too unable to cope. Maybe if I had more faith, more strength, more resilience, I would be able to handle this better. Maybe everyone else knew something I did not, some secret to moving through loss without falling apart.

It wasn't.

There was nothing wrong with me. What I was experiencing was not a personal failure. It was not a lack of faith or strength or coping skills.

What I was experiencing was grief shaped by culture, history, faith, and silence. Grief that carried the weight of being strong for everyone else. Grief that had no safe space to land. Grief that was expected to be private, dignified, contained, even as it threatened to consume me from the inside out.

It was grief that looked different because my experience was different. Because the context I was grieving in, the expectations placed on me, the resources available to me, the support systems I had access to, all of these were shaped by my identity as a Black woman. And the mainstream models of grief did not account for any of that.

The losses of both my parents, all my grandparents, and countless other family and friends, all before I turned twenty-nine, did more than break my heart. They revealed the gaps in how we understand grief in Black communities. Every loss showed me how much pain goes unseen when research does not include us, when clinicians are not trained to hear us, when our stories remain untold, when our grief is pathologized instead of understood.

Every funeral showed me how we perform strength even in our sorrow. How we dress up, show up, hold ourselves together. How we sing songs of praise through our tears. How we cook food for the repast even while our hearts are breaking. How we make sure everyone else is okay before we tend to our own wounds.

Every repast revealed how we feed bodies but not souls. How we gather around tables laden with macaroni and cheese, fried chicken, collard greens, and sweet potato pie. How we eat and laugh and tell stories about the person we lost. But how we rarely talk about the depth of our pain. How we rarely ask each other, "How are you really doing? Not how you are supposed to be doing, but how are you actually feeling right now?"

Every "they're in a better place" reminded me that we comfort others with the same phrases that leave us feeling empty and unheard. We say the things we are supposed to say. We offer the comfort we are supposed to offer. But underneath those well-worn phrases is a grief that remains unspoken, a pain that has no outlet, a sorrow that we carry alone.

This chapter is not just about what I lost. It is about what I found.

I found that grief can become a calling. That the very thing that broke me open could also become the door through which I learned to help others. That my pain was not meaningless, not wasted, not something to be ashamed of or hidden away. It was, instead, the foundation for understanding, for empathy, for a deep commitment to ensuring that others did not have to grieve alone the way I had grieved alone.

I found that pain can create purpose. That the questions I asked in my darkest moments, "Why is no one talking about this? Why does no one understand? Why am I so alone?" could become the foundation for something larger than my individual sorrow. They could become the driving force behind research, advocacy, education. They could become the reason I dedicated my life to studying grief in Black communities, to amplifying voices that had been silenced, to creating the resources I had desperately needed but never found.

I found that my story, once something I tried to hide, something I mentioned only when necessary, something I carried with shame and silence, could become a bridge for others who feel alone in their sorrow. That by speaking what had been unspoken, by naming what had been invisible, I could create the representation I had desperately needed but never found.

I learned that vulnerability is not weakness. That sharing my story, as painful as it is, can create space for others to share theirs. That when one person breaks the silence, it gives permission for others to do the same. That my willingness to say, "this is hard" and "I am struggling" and "I do not have all the answers" could be more healing than any pretense of having it all together.

This book exists because of those losses.
Because of the silence that followed.
Because of the healing that is still unfolding.
And because our grief deserves to be seen.

Not explained away. Not minimized. Not compared to someone else's journey or measured against someone else's timeline. Not dismissed with platitudes or spiritual bypassing or expectations that we should be "over it" by now.

Seen. Honored. Held.

Our grief deserves space to breathe, to move, to exist without apology. It deserves acknowledgment that goes beyond "I'm sorry for your loss" to a deeper understanding of what loss means in the context of our lives, our histories, our communities. It deserves research that includes us, clinicians who understand us, frameworks that reflect the complexity of our experiences.

This is where we begin.

Not with answers, because I do not have all the answers. Not with a roadmap, because grief does not follow a straight path. But with acknowledgment. With honesty. With a commitment to telling the truth about what grief looks and feels like for those of us who have been told to suffer in silence.

This is where we begin, together, in the hope that none of us will have to grieve alone again.

Chapter 2:

Why Black Grief Looks Different

Grief does not live in a vacuum. It lives in history, in culture, in memory, and in the stories we inherit long before we experience our first loss.

To understand Black grief, we must first understand the weight our communities have been carrying for generations. Our pain is not only personal, it is collective. It is shaped by centuries of survival, by resilience born out of necessity, and by a legacy of being told to endure what should never have been endured.

From slavery to segregation, from ongoing racial violence to everyday discrimination, Black communities have learned how to keep moving even when hearts are breaking. We learned to make space for everyone else's pain while often minimizing our own. Strength became our language, even when what we needed was permission to rest.

This history does not disappear when we lose someone we love. It shows up in how we grieve.

For many of us, grief is quiet. It happens behind closed doors and whispered prayers. We cry alone. We hold ourselves together in public and fall apart in private. We are praised for our resilience, yet rarely asked about our pain. And over time, silence becomes the expectation.

The quietness of our grief is not natural. It is learned. Passed down through generations who understood that showing too much emotion could be dangerous, that vulnerability could be weaponized, that survival sometimes meant swallowing sorrow and presenting a face of strength to a world that was already looking for reasons to diminish us.

Our grandmothers and great-grandmothers grieved silently because they had to. Because there was work to do, mouths to feed, children to protect. Because the luxury of falling apart was not afforded to people who were still fighting to be seen as fully human. Because grief, like so much else, became something we learned to carry without complaint.

And so, we inherited this silence. We learned it in the spaces between words; in the way our elders compressed their pain into tight smiles and redirected conversations. We learned it in church, where testimony was expected to end in praise, where struggle was meant to be temporary, where suffering was supposed to lead quickly to salvation. We learned it at kitchen tables and on front porches, where stories were told about those who "made it through" without ever talking about what it cost them to survive.

In our families and churches, strength is often framed as faith. "Be strong," "pray through it," "God will make a way." These words are meant to comfort, but they can also close the door to honest grief. When sorrow is rushed toward spiritual resolution, there is little space to sit in the ache.

Faith becomes a double-edged sword. On one hand, it provides genuine comfort, a framework for meaning making, a community of support. On the other hand, it can become a tool for silencing, a way to bypass the hard work of grieving by jumping straight to acceptance. "God needed another angel" may soothe the speaker, but it rarely soothes the one who is left behind, reaching for a loved one who is no longer there.

The pressure to be strong in faith means that doubt becomes dangerous. Questions become evidence of weakness. Anger at God becomes something to confess rather than something to express. We learn to perform certainty even when we are drowning in confusion. We testify about God's goodness even when we cannot feel it. We praise through pain because that is what is expected, what is modeled, what earns us the nods of approval from those who are watching to see how well we endure.

This framework is not unique to Black communities, but it carries particular weight in spaces where faith has been the primary survival mechanism for generations. Where belief in a better tomorrow, whether in this life or the next, has been the thing that kept people going when everything else said to give up. Where church has been sanctuary, meeting place, organizing hub, and the center of community life.

In these spaces, grief that lingers too long or looks too messy can be seen as a failure of faith, so we shorten our mourning. We dry our tears. We return to service before we are ready, because to stay away too long might suggest that our faith was not strong enough to carry us through.

Black grief is also shaped by mistrust, mistrust of systems that have historically failed us. Many of us hesitate to seek therapy or professional support because we fear being misunderstood, judged, or pathologized. Too often, our emotional expressions are labeled as anger, resistance, or instability rather than pain.

This mistrust is not paranoia. It is pattern recognition.

It is the awareness that mental health systems were not built with us in mind. That the research informing therapeutic practices rarely included Black participants. That the diagnostic criteria for depression, anxiety, and trauma were developed based on white, middle-class experiences and may not accurately capture how these conditions manifest in our communities.

It is the knowledge that Black people have been subjected to unethical medical experimentation, from the Tuskegee syphilis study to the exploitation of Henrietta Lacks' cells. That our bodies and our pain have been used without our consent, without our knowledge, without regard for our humanity. That this history creates a reasonable wariness when it comes to trusting institutions that claim to want to help.

It is the lived experience of walking into therapists' offices and having to educate them about racism, about micro aggressions, about what it means to navigate the world in a Black body. Of having our trauma responses read as personality disorders. Of being medicated when what we needed was to be heard. Of having our grief minimized or misunderstood because the person across from us had no framework for understanding the cumulative weight of racism, loss, and survival.

And so many of us choose to suffer in silence rather than risk being further harmed by systems that claim to heal. We turn to our communities instead, to the people who understand without needing explanation. But even there, we often find the same messages: be strong, pray harder, keep moving forward.

And yet, within our communities, there is also deep wisdom. We know how to gather. We know how to hold each other. We know how to sing, pray, cook, and remember. Our grief is layered with love, memory, and meaning.

When someone dies in a Black community, the response is immediate and collective. Food appears at the door before the family even thinks to ask. People show up to sit with the bereaved, to fill the silence, to keep them from being alone with their pain. Phone trees activate. Church mothers mobilize. Balloon releases are arranged in parks. Memorials are set up on street corners. T-shirts with the name of our loved one circulate, turning grief into something visible, wearable, public. The community wraps itself around the grieving family like a blanket.

There is beauty in this. There is profound wisdom in knowing that grief is not meant to be carried alone, that the first response to loss should be presence, that sometimes the most healing thing is a kitchen full of people who loved the one you lost and are willing to speak their name.

We know how to create rituals that honor both sorrow and celebration. Our funerals are not quiet, somber affairs. They are homegoings, celebrations of life, spaces where tears and laughter can coexist. Where we can mourn the loss and celebrate the legacy in the same breath. Where we can sing songs that acknowledge both the pain of separation and the hope of reunion.

We know how to keep people alive through storytelling. At repasts, around dinner tables, during family gatherings, we tell the stories. We remember the way they laughed, the things they used to say, the meals they cooked, the wisdom they shared. We keep them present through memory, through naming, through refusing to let death have the final word.

This wisdom is real. It is valuable. It is worth preserving and honoring.

But it exists alongside practices that can also silence grief. The same community that shows up with food may not show up with space for ongoing sorrow. The same church that fills the sanctuary for the funeral may grow uncomfortable if grief extends past what feels like an acceptable timeline. The same family that tells stories at the repast may change the subject when someone tries to talk about how much they are still struggling six months, a year, five years later.

What makes Black grief different is not that we feel more, it is that we carry more.

We carry our own losses alongside the inherited grief of those who came before us. We carry stories of survival, strength, and sorrow that were never fully acknowledged. And we carry the hope that healing can look different than what we have been shown.

Every loss we experience is connected to a longer history of loss. When a Black mother buries her son, she is not only grieving her child. She is grieving all the Black sons who have been taken too soon, all the mothers throughout history who have stood where she is standing, all the futures that will never be. Her grief carries echoes.

When a Black family loses someone to illness, they are not only mourning that individual death. They are confronting a healthcare system that has failed Black people for generations, that offers substandard care, that dismisses our pain, that allows preventable deaths because Black lives have not been valued the same as white lives. Their grief is compounded by injustice.

When a community gathers for yet another funeral, they are not only saying goodbye to one person. They are carrying the cumulative weight of violence, poverty, systemic neglect, and premature death that has marked Black life in America since the beginning. Their grief is collective.

This is what it means to carry more. To grieve in a body that holds not just your own sorrow but the sorrow of your ancestors. To mourn in a context where loss is not random but patterned, not individual but structural. To feel the weight of history every time you lose someone you love.

And yet, even as we carry this weight, we are expected to bear it silently. To not name the ways that racism compounds our grief. To not acknowledge that some of our losses were preventable, that some of our pain is the direct result of systems that do not value Black life. To grieve as if our losses exist in a vacuum, separate from the larger context of injustice and inequality.

We are told to focus on the individual, to work through our personal grief, to find our own peace. But how do you find personal peace when your grief is tangled up with collective trauma? How do you work through individual loss when the conditions that caused that loss continue to harm others in your community? How do you heal when the wound keeps being reopened?

These are the questions that mainstream grief models do not address. These are the complexities that get lost when we try to fit Black grief into frameworks that were never designed for us.

Recognizing this is not about victimhood, it is about truth. It is about honoring the full context of our pain so that our healing can be just as deep.

To name the ways that Black grief is different is not to claim that we are uniquely damaged or that our pain is more important than anyone else's. It is simply to insist on accuracy. To refuse to flatten our experience into something more palatable, more comfortable, more easily digestible for those who do not share our history.

It is to say that if we want healing to be real and lasting, it must begin with truth. Truth about what we have endured. Truth about what we continue to endure. Truth about the ways that grief lives in our bodies, our communities, our histories.

And truth about the fact that healing, like grief, does not happen in a vacuum. It happens in community. It happens when we create spaces where all our pain can be spoken. It happens when we develop models of care that account for the fullness of our experience. It happens when we stop pretending that grief is only personal and start acknowledging that it is also political, cultural, historical, and collective.

This truth-telling is not comfortable. It requires us to sit with realities that are painful, that implicate systems we may have believed in, that challenge narratives we have been told about progress and equality. It requires us to acknowledge that we are not okay, that our communities are not okay, that the grief we carry is not only about the people we have lost but about the conditions under which we lost them.

But discomfort is not the same as harm. And truth, even painful truth, is the foundation for real healing.

Our grief deserves language. Our grief deserves care. Our grief deserves to be seen.

It deserves language that can hold its complexity. Words that can name not just sadness but rage, not just sorrow but exhaustion, not just loss but betrayal. Language that can articulate the difference between grief that comes from natural death and grief that comes from preventable death. Between mourning an elder who lived a full life and mourning a child whose life was cut short by violence or neglect.

It deserves care that is informed by cultural competency, that understands the role of faith in our communities without using it to bypass genuine grief work. Care that recognizes the historical reasons for our mistrust and works to earn our trust rather than demanding it. Care that is provided by people who look like us, who understand our experiences, who do not require us to translate our pain into language they can understand.

It deserves to be seen in all its dimensions. Not reduced to stereotypes about strength and resilience. Not romanticized as if suffering has made us noble. Not pathologized as if our responses to trauma are evidence of dysfunction. But seen clearly, honestly, completely.

Seen as grief that is both like and unlike other grief. That shares the universal human experience of loss while also being shaped by the particular realities of Black life in America. That deserves the same compassion and care extended to all who mourn while also requiring specific attention to the unique factors that shape how we experience and express our pain.

This chapter is an invitation to see Black grief fully. To understand it not as a deviation from some neutral standard but as a valid, coherent response to specific historical and ongoing circumstances. To recognize that the ways we grieve make sense given what we have been taught, what we have experienced, what we have survived.

And it is a call to do better. To create spaces where Black grief can be expressed without shame. To develop resources that reflect our realities. To train clinicians who can hold the complexity of our pain. To build communities where strength does not require silence and faith does not preclude honest lamentation.

Our grief is different. And our healing must be different too.

CHAPTER 3

THE GRIEF NO ONE TEACHES US ABOUT

There is a kind of grief that does not come with pies, sympathy cards, or time off from work.

It is quiet. Invisible. Unnamed.

This is the grief no one teaches us about.

We are taught how to mourn death, but not how to grieve broken dreams. We are prepared for funerals, but not for the slow loss of who we thought we would be. We rarely name the pain of relationships that fade, identities that shift, or futures that never arrive. Yet these losses live in the body just as deeply.

Death is recognized. Death brings rituals. Death activates community support and cultural scripts for how to respond. But what about the losses that do not look like death? What about the grief that has no grave to visit, no obituary to publish, no funeral to attend?

This grief shows up when a marriage ends, not through death but through divorce. When a career you built your identity around disappears. When the church that raised you becomes a place where you no longer feel safe. When your body changes in ways you did not choose and cannot reverse. When mental or physical illness takes away the life you planned to live.

These losses are real. They alter the landscape of who we are. They reshape our understanding of ourselves and our place in the world. And yet, we are rarely given permission to grieve them fully.

In classrooms, in training programs, and in therapy spaces, grief is often treated as a singular event, something with a beginning, a middle, and an end. But real grief is not linear. It returns in waves. It reshapes us over time. And for many, it never fully leaves.

The dominant grief models speak in stages: denial, anger, bargaining, depression, acceptance. As if grief moves in an orderly progression from one phase to the next. As if we can check off boxes on our way to healing. As if acceptance is a destination we arrive at and remain in, rather than a place we visit and leave and return to over and over again.

But anyone who has truly grieved knows this is not how it works. Grief is not a ladder you climb, rung by rung, until you reach the top. It is more like an ocean, with waves that crash over you without warning. Some days the water is calm enough to wade through. Other days you are pulled under, gasping for air, wondering if you will ever reach solid ground again.

And for losses that are not death, this non-linear experience is even more pronounced. Because there is no funeral to mark the end of one chapter and the beginning of another. No clear moment when you can say, "It is over now. I can begin to heal." Instead, there is only the slow unraveling of what was, the gradual recognition that life as you knew it has ended, the ongoing process of learning to live in the aftermath.

For Black communities, this unspoken grief is compounded by expectations to remain strong, productive, and faithful no matter the cost. We are rarely given language for exhaustion, numbness, or emotional disconnection. Instead, we are praised for perseverance, even when it is slowly breaking us.

The same cultural forces that shape how we grieve death also shape how we handle these ambiguous losses. The mandate to be strong does not disappear just because what you lost was not a person. If anything, the pressure intensifies, because at least with death, people understand. They may not give you enough time or space to grieve, but they acknowledge that you are grieving something real.

With these other losses, even that acknowledgment is often absent. When a marriage ends, you may be told to "move on" or "find someone better" before you have had a chance to mourn the future you were building together. When you lose a job, especially in communities where employment is precarious and hard-won, you are expected to immediately start looking for the next one, to not waste time dwelling on what was lost. When your health changes, you are encouraged to "stay positive" and focus on what you can still do, as if acknowledging grief over what you have lost is somehow giving up.

In faith communities, these losses can be even harder to name. Because if God is in control, if everything happens for a reason, then questioning why this happened to you can feel like doubting God's plan. Admitting that you are grieving the life you thought you would have can sound like ingratitude for the life you do have. Expressing anger or confusion about your circumstances can be interpreted as a lack of faith.

So, we learn to smile through the pain. To testify about God's faithfulness even when we feel abandoned. To perform gratitude for what remains while privately mourning what was taken. To carry our unacknowledged grief in silence, adding it to the pile of all the other things we are not supposed to talk about.

This kind of grief shows up in quiet ways. In overworking. In emotional distance. In chronic stress that settles into the body.

Overworking becomes a way to avoid feeling. If you are busy enough, if you fill every moment with tasks and obligations, you do not have to sit with the emptiness. You do not have to face the questions that have no good answers. You do not have to acknowledge how much you have lost.

In Black communities, where work has often been both a source of dignity and a survival mechanism, this tendency to overwork can be particularly pronounced. We have been taught that hard work is the path to stability, to respect, to making a better life for ourselves. And so, when life falls apart, we work harder. We take on extra shifts, extra responsibilities, extra burdens, because staying busy feels safer than standing still.

But overworking is not healing. It is postponement. And eventually, the bill comes due.

Emotional distance becomes another coping mechanism. If you do not let people get too close, they cannot see how much you are struggling. They cannot ask questions you do not want to answer. They cannot offer comfort that only highlights how uncomfortable you are. So, you keep people at arm's length, even the people who love you, even the people who might actually be able to help.

This distance shows up as canceling plans at the last minute. As screening phone calls from friends who just want to check in. As keeping conversations surface-level, deflecting any attempt to go deeper. As building walls around your heart and calling it self-protection when really it is self-isolation.

In communities where vulnerability is already seen as weakness, where asking for help can feel like admitting defeat, this emotional distance becomes almost reflexive. We convince ourselves that we are fine on our own, that we do not need anyone, that showing our pain would be a burden to others. But isolation does not protect us. It only ensures that we suffer alone.

Chronic stress settles into the body when grief has nowhere else to go. The tension in your shoulders that never fully releases. The headaches that come and go without clear cause. The stomach problems that doctors cannot quite explain. The exhaustion that sleep does not fix. The immune system that seems to have stopped working properly.

This is what happens when emotional pain is not processed, when it is pushed down and ignored and minimized. It does not disappear. It relocates. It takes up residence in your muscles, your organs, your nervous system. It becomes the background noise of your existence, the constant hum of distress that you learn to live with because you do not know how to make it stop.

For Black communities, this embodied grief is particularly heavy because it is layered. It is not just your current loss that your body is holding. It is also the historical trauma, the daily microaggressions, the cumulative stress of navigating a world that was not designed for your wellbeing. Your body becomes a storage unit for all the grief you have not been allowed to express, all the pain you have had to smile through, all the losses you have never been given permission to mourn.

It shows up when we cannot explain why we feel heavy, even on good days. When we struggle to feel joy without guilt. When we fear that slowing down means falling apart.

There are days when the heaviness is inexplicable. When objectively, things are fine. You have made it through the worst. You have survived. You are functioning. But inside, you feel weighted down, as if you are moving through water, as if every step requires more energy than you have to give.

People ask what is wrong, and you do not know how to answer. Because nothing is wrong, exactly. And yet everything feels wrong. Because you are grieving losses you cannot name, mourning futures that never materialized, carrying sorrow for things that are not supposed to count as real loss.

Joy becomes complicated when you are holding unacknowledged grief. Even moments that should feel good are tinged with something else. Guilt, maybe, because how can you be happy when there is so much you have lost? Or fear, because if you let yourself feel good, you might have to acknowledge how bad you have been feeling. Or numbness, because you have spent so long protecting yourself from pain that you have also shut out the capacity for pleasure.

So, you find yourself unable to fully enjoy anything. You are present but not really there. You smile but do not feel it. You go through the motions of participating in your life without actually being in your life.

Underneath it all is the fear that if you slow down, if you stop moving, if you allow yourself to really feel what you are feeling, you will fall apart completely. That the grief you have been holding at bay will overwhelm you. That once you start crying, you will not be able to stop. That acknowledging the depth of your pain will mean you can never go back to functioning, to coping, to getting through the day.

This fear keeps you running. It keeps you busy and distracted and disconnected. It keeps you from the very thing that could actually help: stopping long enough to tend to your wounds.

And because it has no clear name, we often believe it is a personal failure rather than a human response to loss.

When your grief does not fit the expected mold, when it does not come with sympathy cards and meatloaf, when people do not automatically understand what you are going through, it is easy to conclude that something is wrong with you.

You start to wonder if you are making too big a deal out of things. If you should be over it by now. If other people handle these kinds of losses better and you are just weak or broken or too sensitive.

You compare your invisible grief to other people's visible grief and find yourself lacking. You think, "At least I did not lose someone to death," and feel guilty for struggling when others have it worse. Or you think, "Other people go through divorce and move on," and wonder why you cannot seem to do the same.

This self-blame is perhaps the cruelest part of ambiguous loss. Not only are you grieving, but you are also judging yourself for grieving. Not only are you in pain, but you are also telling yourself that your pain does not count, that it is not legitimate, that you should be able to handle it better.

In Black communities, where we are already conditioned to minimize our pain, to not take up space with our suffering, to prioritize everyone else's needs above our own, this tendency to invalidate our own grief is even stronger. We have internalized the message that our pain does not matter unless it meets certain criteria. And losses that are not death rarely meet those criteria.

So, we suffer in silence. We carry grief that has no name. We endure pain that we cannot explain. And we believe, wrongly, that this is just how it has to be.

The truth is, we are grieving more than we realize.

We grieve safety.
We grieve stability.
We grieve the versions of ourselves we never had the chance to become.

We grieve the feeling of being safe in our own bodies, in our own communities, in the world. The sense that we can relax our guard, that we do not always have to be vigilant, that harm is not waiting around every corner. For many, this safety is something we never had in the first place. But we grieve it nonetheless, grieve the absence of something we deserved but were never given.

We grieve stability, economic and otherwise. The ability to plan for a future, to save money, to build something lasting. In communities where jobs are precarious, where housing is unstable, where one emergency can derail everything, stability is always fragile. And when it is lost, whether through layoffs, evictions, or any number of other crises, the grief is profound. Because it is not just about losing what you had. It is about losing the hope that you might finally, finally have solid ground beneath your feet.

We grieve the versions of ourselves we never had the chance to become. The person you might have been if you had not had to grow up so fast, if you had not had to be strong all the time, if you had been given space to be soft and vulnerable and still loved. The dreams you set aside because survival was more pressing than self-actualization. The talents you never developed because you were too busy working to keep a roof over your head. The relationships you never pursued because you could not afford to be distracted from the work of staying alive.

These are real losses. They deserve to be mourned. They deserve to be named and acknowledged and given space in our hearts.

We grieve opportunities that were foreclosed before we even knew they existed. Education that was out of reach. Careers that were never presented as options. Places we could not go, things we could not do, experiences we could not have, not because we did not want them but because the world did not make space for us to want them.

We grieve the childhood we did not get to have. The innocence that was taken too soon. The play that was replaced with responsibility. The lightness that was weighed down by adult concerns. For those who had to parent their parents, who had to raise their siblings, who had to be strong for everyone around them before they were old enough to know what strength actually meant, there is grief in recognizing what was asked of you and what you were never given in return.

We grieve the relationships that could not survive the weight we were carrying. Friendships that faded because we had nothing left to give. Romantic partnerships that ended because we could not be vulnerable, could not trust, could not believe that love might be safe. Family connections that frayed under the pressure of trauma and misunderstanding and all the things we could not say to each other.

We grieve the person we were before trauma, before loss, before we learned to see the world as dangerous and ourselves as expendable. There is a particular ache in remembering who you used to be, in recognizing how much has changed, in knowing you can never go back.

And we grieve the futures we imagined that will never come to pass. The life we thought we would have by now. The person we thought we would be. The family we thought we would build. The security we thought we would achieve. The peace we thought we would find.

All of these are losses. All of them deserve to be grieved.

Until we learn to name these losses, they will continue to shape us silently. Healing begins when we allow ourselves to acknowledge what has been taken, and to honor the pain that remains.

Naming is the first step. Before we can heal, we must be able to say what hurts. We must develop language for losses that do not have ready-made vocabulary. We must insist that our grief counts, even when it does not fit conventional categories.

This naming is not self-pity. It is not wallowing. It is not making excuses. It is truth-telling. It is refusing to minimize our own experience. It is claiming the right to feel what we feel without shame or apology.

For Black communities, this naming carries particular significance. Because we have been told for so long to be silent about our pain. Because we have been conditioned to believe that our suffering does not matter unless it is extreme. Because we have learned to compare our struggles to those of our ancestors and conclude that we have no right to complain.

But our ancestors did not survive what they survived so that we could continue to suffer in silence. They endured so that we might have better. And part of having better is having the freedom to acknowledge our pain, to name our losses, to grieve what we have endured without constantly having to justify whether it is "bad enough" to warrant attention.

Once we name these losses, we can begin to tend to them. We can create space for grief that does not come with rituals. We can honor pain that does not have a timeline. We can sit with sorrow that does not resolve neatly.

We can give ourselves permission to grieve relationships that ended, even if no one died. To mourn dreams that will not be realized, even if we are still alive to dream new ones. To acknowledge the weight of living with chronic illness, chronic stress, chronic uncertainty, even if we have learned to function despite it.

We can stop waiting for permission from others to validate our grief. We can stop comparing our pain to other people's pain and judging whether ours is significant enough. We can stop performing strength when what we need is to fall apart in the safety of people who will not judge us for breaking.

Healing begins when we allow ourselves to acknowledge what has been taken. When we stop pretending we are fine. When we recognize that the heaviness we carry has a source, that the numbness we feel is a response to pain, that the exhaustion that will not lift is our body's way of saying "this is too much."

Acknowledging does not mean the pain disappears.   It means we stop fighting it. We stop judging ourselves for feeling it. We create space for it to exist alongside everything else we are carrying.

And healing continues when we honor the pain that remains. When we understand that some grief does not resolve, it only changes shape. When we accept that we may carry certain losses for the rest of our lives, and that carrying them does not mean we are broken or weak or stuck.

It means we are human. It means we loved something or someone or some version of ourselves deeply enough that losing it left a mark. And that mark is not something to be ashamed of. It is evidence of our capacity to care, to hope, to imagine better.

This is the grief no one taught us about.
But it is the grief we must learn to face.

Not because facing it will make it go away. But because refusing to face it only gives it more power. Because unacknowledged grief does not fade, it festers. Because the losses we do not mourn become the wounds that never heal.

We must learn to face this grief with honesty and compassion. To look directly at what we have lost without turning away. To feel the full weight of it without collapsing under it. To understand that we can hold both grief and hope, both sorrow and joy, both the pain of what was lost and the possibility of what might still be.

This facing is not a one-time event. It is an ongoing practice. Some days we will be able to look our grief in the eye and sit with it calmly. Other days it will overwhelm us, and the best we can do is survive it. Both responses are valid. Both are part of the process.

We must learn to face it together. To create spaces where ambiguous loss can be named and honored. To build communities that do not require our grief to look a certain way or fit a certain timeline. To develop language and rituals and support systems for losses that have traditionally been invisible.

This is how we begin to heal. Not by minimizing what we have lost. Not by rushing toward resolution. Not by performing strength we do not feel.

But by naming our grief.
By honoring it.
By insisting that it matters.
And by refusing to carry it alone.

CHAPTER 4:

FAITH, SILENCE AND STREGNTH

For many of us, faith is the first language we learn for survival. Long before we understand theology, we understand prayer. Before we can articulate grief, we are taught how to endure. In Black communities, faith is not simply belief, it is inheritance. It is how we made it through what was never meant to be survived.

Faith is woven into the fabric of our communities. It is in the songs our mothers sang while cooking Sunday dinner. It is in the prayers that opened every family gathering, every important conversation, every moment of crisis. It is in the church buildings that served as more than houses of worship, that became schools and meeting places and sanctuaries in the most literal sense.

Our ancestors turned to faith when they had nothing else to turn to. When they were stolen from their homelands and forced into bondage, when their families were torn apart, when their humanity was denied, when their bodies were broken and their spirits were tested beyond measure, faith became the thing that sustained them. It became the belief that there was something beyond the suffering, something that their oppressors could not touch, something that promised that this world's cruelty was not the final word.

This faith has been passed down through generations. It is part of our spiritual DNA, embedded in how we understand ourselves and our place in the world. It is the source of our resilience, our creativity, our ability to find joy even in the midst of sorrow. It is what has allowed us to survive and, against all odds, to thrive.

But sometimes, the very place that teaches us hope also teaches us how to hide.

The same faith that sustained our ancestors through unimaginable suffering also taught them to endure in silence. To not name their pain too loudly, because doing so could bring more harm. To not show their grief too openly, because vulnerability could be weaponized. To testify about God's goodness even when their circumstances were devastating, because maintaining hope was essential to survival.

And so, faith became intertwined with silence. With the suppression of certain emotions. With the performance of strength even when breaking apart inside. These were survival strategies, ways of protecting the self and the community in contexts where showing too much pain could literally be dangerous.

But what was once a necessary adaptation has become a legacy we inherit without always understanding its origins. We learn the scripts without learning the context. We repeat the patterns without questioning whether they still serve us.

We are told to "trust God," to "pray through it," to "be strong." These words are offered with love, yet they can also become walls. They can rush us toward healing before we have even acknowledged what has been broken. They can suggest that faith and grief cannot coexist, when in reality, grief is often where faith is most honest.

"Trust God" can be a genuine invitation to faith. But it can also be a way of shutting down difficult conversations. When someone shares their pain and is immediately told to trust God, the message, intended or not, is that the pain itself is the problem. That if they had more faith, they would not be struggling. That their grief is evidence of spiritual deficiency.

"Pray through it" suggests that prayer is a bridge from suffering to resolution, a tool for getting past grief rather than a space for sitting with it. It implies that the goal is to move through the pain as quickly as possible, to emerge on the other side transformed and testimony ready. But what if the praying through is not about getting to the other side? What if it is about learning to be present in the pain, to bring it before God honestly, to not pretend we are okay when we are not?

"Be strong" is perhaps the most complicated of all. Because strength is valued in our communities for good reason. It has been necessary. It has been lifesaving. It has been the difference between survival and destruction. But when strength becomes the only acceptable response to suffering, when it is used to silence grief rather than support it, it stops being helpful and starts being harmful.

Strength that does not allow for vulnerability is not strength. It is armor. And armor, while protective, is also isolating. It keeps threats out, but it also keeps connection out. It creates distance between us and the people who love us, between us and our own emotions, between us and the God we claim to trust.

These words, "trust God," "pray through it," "be strong," are meant to comfort. The people who offer them are not trying to cause harm. They are sharing what they have been taught, what has been passed down to them, what they genuinely believe will help. But impact is not the same as intent. And the impact of these words, particularly when they are offered prematurely or used to redirect grief rather than hold it, can be isolating and shaming.

They can rush us toward healing before we have even acknowledged what has been broken. Before we have named the loss. Before we have sat with the reality of what we are facing. They skip over the necessary work of lament and move straight to resolution, as if grief is an inconvenient detour on the way to testimony rather than a legitimate destination in its own right.

They can suggest that faith and grief cannot coexist. That if you are truly faithful, you should not be this sad, this angry, this confused. That grief is a sign of weak faith rather than a natural response to loss. That praising God and crying over what you have lost are mutually exclusive rather than intimately connected.

When in reality, grief is often where faith is most honest.

The faith that does not allow for questions is not deep faith. It is fragile faith, faith that cannot bear the weight of real human experience. The faith that insists on certainty is not mature faith. It is shallow faith, faith that has not been tested by genuine suffering.

Real faith, the kind that sustains us through the darkest valleys, is faith that can hold complexity. Faith that can say "I believe" and "I am struggling" in the same breath. Faith that can praise God on Sunday and rage at God on Monday. Faith that can testify about divine goodness while also naming earthly pain.

This is the faith we see in Scripture, in the psalms of lament, in Job's complaints, in Jeremiah's weeping, in Jesus' cry from the cross. It is faith that is honest about suffering. Faith that does not pretend everything is fine when it is not. Faith that brings the full weight of human anguish before a God who is big enough to handle it.

But this is not always the faith we are taught in our communities. Too often, we are taught a sanitized version, a faith that jumps from struggle to resolution without lingering in the messy middle. A faith that focuses on the testimony, the breakthrough, the miracle, without honoring the long, hard process of getting there.

We are taught to end our prayers with praise, to conclude our laments with affirmations of God's goodness, to tie everything up neatly with a bow of faith. And while there is value in choosing praise, in actively remembering God's faithfulness, in looking for hope even in dark times, there is also danger when this becomes mandatory rather than voluntary. When it becomes a performance rather than a genuine expression of faith.

Early learning taught that strength was expected, not questioned. That crying should be brief. That sadness should be quiet. That healing meant moving forward quickly. And when we could not move on, we wondered if something was wrong with us, or worse, with our faith.

These expectations are absorbed long before we can articulate them. We learn them by watching the adults around us, by observing who gets praised and who gets questioned, by noticing which emotions are welcomed and which are shut down.

We learn that certain displays of grief are acceptable, and others are not. That tears at a funeral are expected but tears six months later are excessive. That anger is never okay, especially not anger at God. That doubt is dangerous, a slippery slope that leads away from faith. That the only acceptable narrative is the one that ends in triumph.

We learn that strength means not falling apart. That it means showing up, functioning, continuing to serve even when our hearts are breaking. That it means being the rock for others, the one people can depend on, the one who holds it together when everyone else is coming undone.

And we learn that deviating from these expectations has consequences. Not always explicit ones, not always punitive, but consequences, nonetheless. The subtle pulling away of community support. The well-meaning suggestions that we need to pray more, have more faith, trust God better. The questions about whether we are taking care of ourselves spiritually, as if our ongoing grief is evidence of spiritual neglect.

So, when we find ourselves unable to move on, unable to be strong in the expected ways, unable to testify about breakthrough when we are still in the breaking, we internalize the message that we are failing. Failing at grief, failing at faith, failing at being the kind of person our community needs us to be.

And this failure feels deeply personal. We do not recognize it as a problem with the system, with the expectations placed on us, with the narrow definitions of acceptable grief. Instead, we conclude that something is wrong with us. That we are too weak, too faithless, too broken to heal the way we are supposed to heal.

This self-blame compounds the grief. We are not only mourning our loss, but we are also mourning our perceived failure to mourn correctly. We are not only carrying our pain, but we are also carrying shame about that pain. We are grieving and judging ourselves for grieving, suffering and condemning ourselves for suffering.

But grief does not disappear when we spiritualize it.   It simply goes underground.

Telling someone to pray through their grief without also creating space for them to feel their grief does not eliminate the grief. It only teaches them to hide it. To perform faith while privately falling apart. To smile in church while crying in the car on the way home.

Grief that is not expressed does not evaporate. It relocates. It finds other outlets, other ways to make itself known.

It shows up in exhaustion that prayer alone does not relieve. In anger we feel ashamed to name. In bodies that carry stress like a second skin. When grief is not given language, it finds expression elsewhere.

The exhaustion is bone deep. It is the fatigue that comes from constantly performing, from holding up a facade of being okay when you are not okay. It is the weariness of split living, of presenting oneself to the world while being an entirely different self in private. Prayer can be comforting, prayer can provide moments of peace, but prayer alone cannot fix the exhaustion that comes from denying your own reality.

The anger is complicated by shame. Because we have been taught that anger, especially at God, is wrong. That it is evidence of insufficient faith, of spiritual immaturity, of not understanding God's plan. So, when we feel angry, we try to suppress it. We try to pray it away, to reframe it, to transform it into something more acceptable. But suppressed anger does not disappear. It turns inward, becoming depression, self-blame, bitterness. Or it leaks out sideways, showing up as irritability with the people around us, as snapping at small inconveniences, as a general sense of being on edge.

The body keeps score. Shoulders carry tension. Jaws clench during sleep. Stomachs churn with unnamed anxiety. Headaches appear with alarming frequency. The immune system weakens under the constant strain. Chronic pain conditions develop or worsen. Sleep becomes difficult, either too little or too much, neither restful.

This is what happens when grief is spiritualized but not actually processed. When we are told to give it to God without being taught how to sit with it ourselves. When we are encouraged to fast and pray but discouraged from therapy or other forms of support. When faith is positioned as the only necessary tool for healing, rather than one valuable tool among many.

Faith was never meant to silence us. In Scripture, lament is not a failure of belief, it is an act of trust. It is saying, "I am hurting, and I am still here." Healing begins when we allow ourselves to bring our whole selves before God, not just the parts that look strong.

The Bible is full of lament. More than a third of the psalms are psalms of lament, prayers that cry out in pain, that question God's presence, that demand answers, that refuse to prettify suffering. The book of Lamentations is an entire text dedicated to grief. Job spends chapter after chapter expressing his anguish and confusion. Jeremiah is known as the weeping prophet. Jesus himself wept openly and cried out in agony.

Scripture does not model silent suffering. It models honest, raw, unfiltered expression of pain brought before a God who can handle it. It shows us people who trust God enough to bring their real feelings, their real questions, their real struggles to God in prayer.

Lament is an act of faith precisely because it assumes that God is present and listening. That God cares about our suffering. That we can bring our whole selves, not just our put-together selves, into God's presence. It is more faithful to cry out to God in anger and confusion than to perform praise while privately pulling away.

True lament says, "I am hurting, and I am still here."

It acknowledges the pain without denying the relationship. It expresses the anguish without abandoning the connection. It creates space for both grief and faith to coexist.

This is the kind of faith that leads to healing. Not the performative faith that insists everything is fine when it is not. Not the shallow faith that cannot tolerate difficult emotions. But the deep, honest, sometimes messy faith that brings everything into the light, that refuses to hide, that trusts that God is big enough to handle our humanity.

Healing begins when we allow ourselves to bring our whole selves before God. Not just the parts that look strong, not just the emotions that seem appropriate, not just the questions that have easy answers. But all of it. The doubt and the faith. The anger and the hope. The despair and the clinging to something beyond the despair.

When we can pray from a place of honesty rather than performance, when we can come before God as we are rather than as we think we should be, that is when transformation becomes possible. Not because the pain immediately disappears, but because we are no longer carrying the additional burden of pretending it does not exist.

True faith makes room for tears.

Faith that is worth having is faith that can hold our sorrow. That does not rush us past our pain. That does not shame us for not being over it yet. That understands that crying is not the opposite of trusting God but sometimes the most honest form of prayer we have.

The God who created us with tear ducts is not surprised or offended when we use them. The God who gave us the capacity for grief is not disappointed when we grieve. The faith that tells us to suppress our tears is not protecting God's reputation. It is protecting our own discomfort with emotion.

Making room for tears means creating spaces where crying is not seen as weak, where sadness is not rushed toward resolution, where people can fall apart and be held rather than fixed. It means training our church leaders to sit with suffering rather than immediately trying to solve it. It means preaching sermons that honor lament alongside praise.

It means changing our language, our practices, our expectations. It means saying "I am here with you" more often than "everything will be okay." It means praying with people in their pain rather than for their pain to immediately disappear. It means trusting that God is present in the grief, not just on the other side of it.

True strength allows us to rest.

The strength we need is not the strength that never breaks. It is the strength to break and then keep breathing. The strength to admit we cannot do it alone. The strength to ask for help. The strength to stop performing and start being honest.

Rest is not weakness. It is wisdom. It is the recognition that we are human, that we have limits, that pushing past those limits does not make us strong, it makes us sick. It is the practice of trusting that the world will keep turning even if we step back for a moment. That we do not have to earn our worth through constant productivity and service.

In communities where rest has often been a luxury we could not afford, where stopping has meant falling behind, where exhaustion has been a badge of honor, learning to rest is revolutionary. It requires unlearning everything we have been taught about our value being tied to our output. It requires believing that we are worthy of care even when we are not functioning at full capacity.

Allowing ourselves to rest is an act of faith. It is trusting that God's grace is sufficient, that we do not have to earn love through performance, that we can be still and know that we are held. It is releasing the belief that our worth is determined by our strength and embracing the truth that we are beloved even in our weakness.

This kind of strength, the strength that makes room for tears and rest, is not weakness disguised as strength. It is true strength. The strength that comes from knowing who we are, including our limitations. The strength that comes from being honest rather than pretending. The strength that comes from community rather than isolation.

It is the strength our ancestors had when they sang songs of freedom while still in bondage. When they maintained hope without denying their reality. When they held onto faith not by suppressing their pain but by bringing it into their prayers, their songs, their testimonies.

We honor that legacy not by repeating their suffering or their silence, but by claiming the freedom they fought for. The freedom to grieve honestly. The freedom to express our full humanity. The freedom to bring all of who we are before God and community without shame.

This is the faith we need. Not the faith that silences. But the faith that liberates. The faith that makes room for our whole selves, tears and strength and everything in between.

CHAPTER 5

WHAT RESEARCH SAYS- AND WHAT IT MISSES

Much of what we know about grief comes from research that does not look like us, sound like us, or live like us. Black experiences are often absent, minimized, or misunderstood within academic spaces. And when data does not include us, the conclusions cannot fully serve us.

The foundations of grief research were built on studies of predominantly white, middle-class populations. The landmark work on stages of grief, the models of bereavement that inform clinical practice, the theories about what constitutes "normal" versus "complicated" grief, all of these emerged from research that rarely included Black participants in meaningful numbers.

This is not accidental. It reflects broader patterns in psychological and medical research, patterns rooted in a history of excluding, exploiting, and pathologizing Black bodies and Black experiences. From the Tuskegee syphilis study to the use of enslaved people for medical experimentation, from the theft of Henrietta Lacks' cells to ongoing disparities in who gets included in clinical trials, the relationship between Black communities and research institutions has been marked by harm and mistrust.

And so, when grief researchers developed their frameworks, when they identified their stages and created their models, they did so without adequately accounting for cultural differences in how grief is expressed, experienced, or understood. They assumed universality where there was actually specificity. They created standards based on particular populations and then applied those standards to everyone, regardless of fit.

The result is a body of knowledge that claims to explain grief universally but actually describes grief particularly. It describes grief as experienced by people who have access to therapy, who can take time off work, who live in communities where emotional expression is encouraged, who can afford to prioritize their mental health, who do not face daily discrimination, who are not carrying generational trauma.

This absence is not neutral. It shapes the way clinicians are trained. It determines which treatment models are considered "evidence based." It influences whose pain is validated and whose is questioned.

When clinicians are trained using research that excludes Black experiences, they learn frameworks that do not account for cultural context. They learn to identify "symptoms" without understanding that what looks like avoidance might be culturally adaptive silence. That what appears to be prolonged grief might be the natural response to cumulative loss. That what seems like resistance to treatment might be well-founded mistrust of systems that have historically caused harm.

They learn intervention strategies developed for and tested on populations that are not representative of the diversity they will encounter in practice. Cognitive behavioral therapy designed for individual emotional processing may not translate well to communities where grief is collective. Exposure-based treatments may not account for ongoing trauma, for the reality that the threat is not past but present. Talk therapy assumes that verbal expression is healing but does not always recognize cultural contexts where other forms of expression, spiritual practices, communal rituals, are more aligned with how healing actually happens.

The designation of certain treatments as "evidence-based" sounds objective, scientific, neutral. But evidence-based according to whom? Based on which evidence? Gathered from which populations? When the evidence base is narrow, when it excludes whole communities, then treatments deemed evidence-based may only be evidence-based for some.

This creates a hierarchy of knowledge where research-validated approaches are privileged over community wisdom, where clinical expertise is valued more highly than lived experience, where what counts as legitimate treatment is determined by studies that did not include the people being treated.

And it influences whose pain is validated and whose is questioned. When grief does not present in the expected ways, when it does not follow the predicted timeline, when it does not respond to the standard interventions, clinicians trained in narrow frameworks may conclude that something is wrong with the griever rather than with the framework.

Black clients may be told their grief is complicated or pathological when it is contextual. They may be diagnosed with disorders when what they are experiencing is a normal response to abnormal circumstances. They may be offered medications to manage symptoms that are not symptoms of illness but signals of unprocessed collective trauma, ongoing discrimination, cultural disconnection.

Their pain is questioned because it does not fit the models. Their coping strategies are pathologized because they do not match the textbook. Their healing is delayed because the tools being offered were not designed for the wounds they carry.

When research does not reflect our realities, we are left to adapt ourselves to systems that were never designed with us in mind. Our grief becomes something to be explained rather than understood. Our coping is labeled dysfunctional instead of contextual.

The burden falls on us to translate our experiences into language that makes sense within dominant frameworks. To explain why the stages of grief do not capture what we are going through. To justify why we are not "better" yet when the timeline suggests we should be. To defend our cultural practices, our spiritual beliefs, our ways of mourning as legitimate rather than primitive or resistant.

We are expected to fit ourselves into boxes that were not built for us. To modify our grief to match what research says grief should look like. To adjust our healing to align with what treatment models say healing should involve. And when we cannot or will not do this, when our experiences refuse to be flattened into the expected shape, we are told that we are the problem.

Our grief becomes something to be explained. Why is it lasting so long? Why does it look like this? Why are you not engaging with treatment the way you are supposed to? The questions are framed as curiosity but often carry judgment. They locate the issue within the individual rather than examining whether the framework itself might be inadequate.

Our coping strategies are labeled dysfunctional. Relying on community instead of individual therapy? Dysfunctional. Turning to spiritual practices instead of clinical interventions? Dysfunctional. Maintaining emotional privacy instead of immediately disclosing? Dysfunctional. The label erases context, erases culture, erases the reality that what counts as functional depends on environment and that strategies that might be maladaptive in one context can be lifesaving in another.

But what if our coping is not dysfunctional but deeply functional for the world we live in? What if silence is not avoidance but protection? What if relying on community is not dependence but wisdom? What if our grief looks different not because we are doing it wrong but because our experiences are different, our histories are different, our contexts are different?

But lived experience is also knowledge.

Research has long privileged certain types of knowledge over others. Quantitative data over qualitative narrative. Experimental studies over observational understanding. Professional expertise over community wisdom. In this hierarchy, lived experience is often dismissed as anecdotal, as unscientific, as less valid than knowledge generated through "rigorous" research methods.

But this dismissal is a form of gatekeeping. It determines who gets to be a knowledge creator and who is merely a subject. Who gets to interpret experiences and who simply provides data to be interpreted by others. Who is seen as an expert and who is seen as a recipient of expertise.

Lived experience is knowledge. It is knowledge that comes from being in the world, from navigating systems, from surviving what was not meant to be survived. It is knowledge that cannot be accessed through surveys or experiments because it is too complex, too nuanced, too contextual to be reduced to variables and measured.

Our stories hold data that cannot be captured in numbers alone. They reveal patterns, cultural truths, and emotional landscapes that statistics overlook. When we are not invited into the research process, our healing becomes secondary.

Stories tell us how grief feels, not how researchers predict it should feel. They show us the texture of loss, the way it changes over time, the moments when it hits hardest, the ways it intersects with other identities and experiences. They reveal that grief is not uniform, that it does not follow neat stages, that it is shaped by context and culture and individual circumstance.

Stories show us patterns that numbers miss. The pattern of how loss accumulates in communities facing chronic violence. The pattern of how mistrust develops when systems repeatedly fail you.

The pattern of how faith sustains and sometimes silences. The pattern of how strength is performed at the cost of wellbeing. These patterns exist in the spaces between data points, in the narratives that connect individual experiences into collective understanding.

Stories preserve cultural truths. They pass down wisdom about how our communities have always dealt with grief, what has helped and what has harmed, which practices honor our values, and which betray them. They remind us that we have our own traditions, our own ways of making meaning, our own resources for healing that existed long before Western psychology claimed authority over human suffering.

Stories map emotional landscapes that statistics cannot chart. The geography of grief in a body that carries historical trauma. The territory of loss in a life marked by ongoing discrimination. The topography of mourning in communities where death comes too often and too young. These landscapes are real, they shape experience profoundly, but they resist quantification.

When we are not invited into the research process, when our stories are not sought out, when our knowledge is not valued, our healing becomes secondary. Research continues to generate findings that do not serve us. Interventions continue to be developed that do not work for us. Resources continue to be allocated to approaches that were not designed with us in mind.

And we are left on the margins, expected to be grateful for whatever scraps of attention we receive, expected to make do with tools that do not fit our hands.

Inclusion is not charity, it is necessity. To understand grief fully, we must center voices that have been historically ignored. Our pain is not an outlier. It is part of the human story.

Inclusion in research is often framed as a diversity initiative, a nice thing to do, an ethical consideration. But it is more fundamental than that. It is a requirement for accurate knowledge. You cannot understand grief comprehensively if you only study grief in some populations. You cannot develop universal models if your data is not universal. You cannot claim to understand the human experience of loss if you exclude whole groups of humans.

Centering voices that have been historically ignored does not mean relegating other voices to the margins. It means expanding the conversation, broadening the understanding, complicating the models in ways that make them more accurate, more useful, more true.

It means asking different questions. Not just "how do people grieve?" but "how do people grieve in contexts of ongoing oppression?" Not just "what helps people heal?" but "what helps people heal when the systems meant to support them have historically harmed them?" Not just "what are the stages of grief?" but "whose experiences informed these stages and whose were excluded?"

It means using different methods. Not only quantitative surveys but also qualitative interviews. Not only clinical observations but also community-based participatory research. Not only expert-led studies but also projects where community members shape the questions, collect the data, interpret the findings.

It means valuing different types of knowledge. Not only what can be measured but also what can be witnessed. Not only what shows up in experiments but also what emerges in conversations. Not only what professionals observe but also what people experiencing grief themselves report.

Our pain is not an outlier. It is not a deviation from the norm. It is not an exception that proves the rule. It is part of the human story, a legitimate expression of human grief, a valid response to human loss.

Treating Black grief as an outlier suggests that there is a normal grief, a standard grief, a grief that is the baseline against which all other grief is measured. And that baseline is presumed to be white grief, grief as experienced in white, middle-class contexts, grief that aligns with Western individualistic models.

But this presumed normal is not actually normal. It is particular. It is one way of grieving among many. And when it is treated as the standard, when everything else is measured against it, then anything that differs gets marked as abnormal, as complicated, as requiring explanation.

Black grief is not abnormal. It is differently normal. It is shaped by different histories, different present realities, different cultural values. It makes sense within its context. And that context must be part of how we understand it, not dismissed as confounding variables but recognized as essential to the experience itself.

And it deserves to be studied with respect.

Respect means approaching Black grief not as a problem to be solved but as an experience to be understood. Not as a pathology to be diagnosed but as a response to be contextualized. Not as a deviation to be corrected but as a reality to be honored.

Respect means listening to what Black people say about their own grief rather than imposing interpretations from the outside. It means trusting that we are the experts on our own experiences, that we know what we are feeling better than researchers who observe us from a distance.

Respect means acknowledging the harm that has been done in the name of research and committing to do better. It means understanding why mistrust exists and working to rebuild trust through transparency, through sharing power, through ensuring that research benefits the communities it studies rather than only the careers of researchers.

Respect means centering community needs in research design. What questions matter to the community? What outcomes would actually improve people's lives? How can research be conducted in ways that honor cultural values rather than violating them? Who should have access to the findings, and how should they be shared?

Respect means compensating people for their time and knowledge. Not treating participation as a favor people do for science but recognizing it as labor that deserves fair payment. Not extracting stories and data from communities without giving anything back.

Respect means using findings to advocate for change. Research that documents disparities without pushing for solutions is incomplete. Research that identifies problems without supporting communities to address them is extractive. The point is not just to understand Black grief but to use that understanding to create better support, to challenge inadequate systems, to build resources that work.

When research is conducted with respect, when it centers Black voices and values Black knowledge, when it is designed to serve Black communities rather than study them, it can be transformative. It can validate experiences that have been dismissed. It can provide evidence for what communities have always known. It can create pressure for systems to change.

But when research continues to exclude, to misinterpret, to pathologize, it perpetuates harm. It reinforces the idea that Black pain does not matter, that Black healing is not a priority, that Black lives and Black losses are less worthy of careful attention.

We deserve better. We deserve research that sees us fully, that honors our experiences, that takes our grief as seriously as it takes anyone else's. We deserve frameworks that were built with us in mind, tools that work for us, knowledge that serves our healing.

And we deserve to be part of creating that knowledge. Not just as subjects but as researchers. Not just as participants but as designers. Not just as people studied but as people studying, interpreting, understanding, and sharing what we learn in ways that benefit our communities.

This is what it means to center Black voices in grief research. Not to add us as an afterthought but to recognize that our experiences are essential to understanding grief itself. That without us, the picture is incomplete. That our stories, our pain, our healing are not marginal but central to the human experience of loss.

And when we are finally included, when our knowledge is finally valued, when our grief is finally studied with the respect it deserves, the entire field will be richer for it. Not just for us, but for everyone. Because understanding grief more fully, in all its cultural complexity, serves all who grieve.

This is the work that needs to be done. And it starts with recognizing what research has missed and committing to do better.

CHAPTER 6:

HISTORICAL TRAUMA, AND COLLECTIVE LOSS

Our grief did not begin with us. It was shaped by generations of loss, some named, many never acknowledged. The pain of our ancestors lives in the spaces between our memories. It echoes in the fears we cannot explain, in the resilience we inherited, and in the grief that feels heavier than a single life.

When we experience loss, we do not grieve in isolation. We grieve in bodies that remember. Bodies that carry the imprint of generations who came before us, who survived what should not have been survived, who endured what should never have been endured. Their survival is our inheritance, but so is their pain.

This is not metaphorical. It is not poetic language describing something abstract. It is increasingly understood as biological reality. Research in epigenetics shows that trauma can alter gene expression, that the effects of severe stress can be passed down through generations, that our bodies carry cellular memories of experiences we never personally lived through.

The children and grandchildren of Holocaust survivors show patterns of stress response similar to survivors themselves. The descendants of people who lived through famine show metabolic changes that reflect their ancestors' starvation. And Black

Americans, descendants of enslaved people, descendants of those who survived the Middle Passage, Jim Crow, lynching, ongoing systemic violence, carry markers of that trauma in their bodies.

This is historical trauma. Trauma that accumulates across generations. Trauma that does not disappear just because time passes. Trauma that shapes how we navigate the world even when we do not consciously know its origins.

Historical trauma is not just something that happened long ago. It is something that continues to shape how we see the world and ourselves. It lives in our bodies, in our family stories, and in the silence passed down like an heirloom.

We carry it in our nervous systems, in the heightened vigilance that feels like anxiety but is a survival mechanism inherited from ancestors who had to constantly scan for danger. In the tendency toward hypervigilance, toward expecting the worst, toward not fully relaxing even in moments of safety. These are not personal failings. They are adaptations that kept our people alive, passed down through generations because they served a purpose in contexts where threat was constant.

We carry it in our cardiovascular systems, in the elevated blood pressure and heart disease rates that cannot be explained by genetics alone but make sense when we account for the cumulative stress of living in bodies that have been targets of violence for centuries. The weathering that happens when you are always on guard, always having to prove your humanity, always navigating systems designed to harm you.

We carry it in our immune systems, in the inflammatory responses that are higher in people who experience chronic discrimination, in the ways that stress literally makes us sick. The body keeping score not just of our own experiences but of our ancestors' experiences, holding trauma that we inherited along with our eye color and our name.

We carry it in our family stories, in the gaps where information should be but is not. In the ancestors we cannot trace because records were not kept, because names were changed, because families were torn apart. In the silences around certain topics, certain histories, certain pains that were never spoken about because speaking about them was too dangerous or too overwhelming.

We carry it in the warnings passed down from parent to child. How to behave around police. How to move through white spaces. How to protect yourself, how to make yourself smaller, how to survive. These lessons are practical, necessary, but they are also transmissions of trauma. They teach us that the world is dangerous for bodies like ours, that we cannot afford to be careless, that survival requires constant vigilance.

And we carry it in the silence, in what we do not talk about because it is too painful, too complicated, too much. The silence around slavery and its ongoing impacts. The silence around losses that were never mourned because there was no time, no space, no permission to mourn. The silence that becomes a family pattern, a cultural norm, a way of protecting ourselves that also cuts us off from healing.

We grieve what was taken.
We grieve what was denied.
We grieve the lives our ancestors never had the chance to live.

What was taken is staggering in its scope. Land, language, culture, family, freedom, dignity, humanity itself. Ancestors stolen from their homelands, forced onto ships where many did not survive the journey, sold into bondage that would last for generations. This is not distant history. This is the foundation on which this country was built, and the reverberations continue.

What was taken includes the ability to keep families together. Parents separated from children, spouses from each other, siblings scattered to different plantations with no way to stay in contact, no way to know if the people they loved were alive or dead. The grief of that separation, the trauma of that rupture, does not disappear just because the people who experienced it directly are no longer living.

What was taken includes names, identities, connections to ancestral homelands. People who were stripped of their names and given new ones by enslavers. People who lost their languages, their spiritual practices, their cultural traditions, not by choice but by force. The grief of cultural erasure, of not knowing where you come from, of having your history begin with your oppression rather than with your rich, complex, whole humanity.

What was taken includes the right to safety, to bodily autonomy, to make choices about your own life. People who were treated as property, whose bodies were violated, whose labor was stolen, who had no legal recourse, no protection, no recognition as fully human. The trauma of that dehumanization runs deep, shapes how descendants see themselves and are seen by the world.

What was denied includes opportunities that should have been available but were not. Education that was illegal for enslaved people, that was segregated and underfunded for their descendants. Economic advancement that was systematically blocked through redlining, discriminatory lending, exclusion from programs like the GI Bill that built white generational wealth. Political power that was suppressed through violence, through voter suppression tactics, through gerrymandering and poll taxes and literacy tests designed to disenfranchise.

What was denied includes the right to grieve. Enslaved people who lost children, parents, partners, and had to keep working, had to show no emotion, had to perform compliance even in the midst of devastating loss. Their grief was denied recognition, denied space, denied validity. And that pattern of denied grief continues, in communities where we are expected to be strong, to move on, to not dwell on pain.

What was denied includes the imagination of different futures. When your present is defined by oppression, when your options are limited by systemic barriers, when your very survival is precarious, the luxury of dreaming big dreams, of imagining lives beyond survival, is often out of reach. We grieve the futures our ancestors deserved but never got to have. The peace they deserved. The joy they deserved. The freedom to simply be.

And we grieve the lives they never had the chance to live. The talents that went undeveloped because there was no opportunity. The contributions that were never made because the door was closed. The relationships that never formed because connection was dangerous. The children who died too young, the elders who did not get to grow old, the countless lives cut short by violence, by preventable illness, by the grinding weight of oppression.

This grief is not always visible, but it is deeply felt. It influences how we love, how we protect ourselves, and how we respond to loss. When one wound is triggered, many others rise with it.

We may not consciously think about historical trauma on a daily basis. We may not wake up each morning thinking about slavery or Jim Crow or the ongoing violence against Black bodies. But it is there, underneath, shaping our responses in ways we might not even recognize.

It influences how we love. The hesitation to get too attached because attachment has meant loss. The fear of letting people in because vulnerability has been dangerous. The tendency to keep moving, to not settle, to maintain escape routes because staying put has historically meant being trapped. The ways we protect our hearts even as we long for connection, the armor we wear even with the people we trust most.

It influences how we protect ourselves. The vigilance that never fully turns off. The scanning for threats that happens automatically. The awareness of exits, of who is around us, of how we are being perceived. The code-switching, the adjusting of behavior based on context, the constant calculation of safety. These are not paranoia. These are survival skills honed over generations.

It influences how we respond to loss. Why a single loss can feel like it is activating every loss that came before it. Why grief can feel disproportionate to the immediate situation, because it is not just about the immediate situation. It is about this loss plus the loss of a parent plus the loss of a grandparent plus the losses they carried plus the losses their parents carried, going back and back and back.

When one wound is triggered, many others rise with it. This is how collective trauma works. A traffic stop is never just a traffic stop when you know the history of Black people and police violence. A health scare is never just a health scare when you know about medical racism and preventable deaths. A job loss is never just a job loss when you understand the fragility of Black economic security.

Each new loss, each new threat, each new injustice activates the old ones. Opens the wounds that were never fully healed. Brings to the surface pain that was buried but not resolved. And suddenly you are not just dealing with what is happening now. You are dealing with everything that happened before to you and to those who came before you.

This can feel overwhelming. It can feel like too much. Because it is too much for any one person to carry. But that is the nature of collective trauma. It is too big for individual processing.

It requires collective acknowledgment, collective witnessing, collective healing.

Healing must honor this collective story. It must acknowledge that some pain was never meant to be carried alone, and that we are still learning how to put it down.

Individual therapy models that focus only on personal history miss the larger context. They try to treat symptoms without addressing root causes. They offer coping strategies for managing pain without acknowledging why the pain is so deep, so persistent, so intergenerational.

Healing from collective trauma requires collective approaches. It requires creating spaces where people can tell their stories and have them witnessed by others who understand. Where the pain of one person is recognized as connected to the pain of the community. Where grief is shared rather than isolated.

It requires acknowledging the full scope of what has been lost and what continues to be lost. Not minimizing it, not rushing past it, not trying to make it palatable for people who are uncomfortable with the weight of it. But naming it fully, honoring it completely, creating room for it to be as big as it is.

It requires recognizing that healing is not linear and not quick. That trauma that took centuries to accumulate will not be resolved in a few therapy sessions. That some wounds run so deep that they may never fully close, and that learning to live with them, to tend them, to not let them define everything but also not ignore them, is its own form of healing.

It requires building community practices that honor both grief and resilience. Rituals that acknowledge loss. Gatherings that create space for lament. Storytelling that preserves memory. Art that gives form to pain. Music that holds both sorrow and hope. These are not luxuries. They are necessities for collective healing.

And it requires acknowledging that some pain was never meant to be carried alone. That trying to heal individually from collective trauma is like trying to bail out a flooding basement with a teaspoon. The scale is wrong. The approach is inadequate. You need a different method, one that matches the magnitude of what you are facing.

We are still learning how to put it down. How to stop carrying trauma that is not ours to carry, that we inherited but do not have to pass on. How to break cycles that have repeated for generations. How to create different futures for the children coming after us.

This is hard work. It requires confronting things we would rather not confront. It requires feeling things we have been taught to suppress. It requires speaking things we have been taught to keep silent. It requires challenging systems that benefit from our silence, from our exhaustion, from our continued carrying of burdens that should never have been placed on us.

But it is possible. Not easy, but possible. We see it in movements for racial justice, in community healing initiatives, in the growing body of work on racial trauma and culturally informed therapy. In the increasing recognition that healing must happen both individually and collectively, that we need both personal tools and systemic change.

We are not broken.
We are remembering.

There is a narrative that trauma breaks people, that those who carry it are damaged, that the legacy of historical trauma makes us less than whole. This narrative is wrong.

We are not broken. We are the descendants of people who survived. Who found ways to maintain their humanity in contexts designed to strip it away. Who created beauty in the midst of horror. Who built families and communities despite every effort to destroy them. Who passed down wisdom and strength and love through generations.

The fact that we are here, that we have survived, that we continue to resist and create and love and hope, is evidence not of brokenness but of profound resilience. Not the toxic kind of resilience that says we should be able to endure anything without complaint. But the real kind, the kind that acknowledges both the wound and the healing, both the trauma and the resistance to it.

We are remembering. Remembering what was done to our ancestors. Remembering the ways trauma shows up in our bodies and our communities. Remembering the coping strategies that were adaptive in their time but may not serve us now. Remembering that we carry not just trauma but also resistance, not just pain but also power.

Remembering is part of healing. We cannot heal what we do not acknowledge. We cannot address trauma we pretend does not exist. We cannot change patterns we do not recognize. Remembering is the first step toward something different.

We remember so that we can grieve what needs to be grieved. So that we can honor what needs to be honored. So that we can release what needs to be released. So that we can transform pain into purpose, trauma into testimony, suffering into solidarity.

We remember not to stay stuck in the past but to understand the present. To see clearly how history shapes our current reality. To recognize that what looks like personal struggle is often the manifestation of collective trauma. To understand that healing ourselves is part of healing our communities, and healing our communities is part of healing ourselves.

We remember for the ancestors who were not allowed to remember, who had their histories erased, who were told to forget where they came from. We remember as an act of resistance, an act of reclamation, an act of honoring those who came before.

And we remember for the children who come after, so that they inherit not just trauma but also truth. Not just pain but also power. Not just grief but also the knowledge that they are part of a lineage of survivors, that they carry the strength of those who endured, that they are connected to something larger than themselves.

Historical trauma is real. It is heavy. It is ongoing. But it does not have the final word.

We have the final word. Through our healing. Through our resistance. Through our refusal to let trauma define us even as we acknowledge its impact. Through our commitment to breaking cycles, to creating new patterns, to building futures where our children do not have to carry what we have carried.

This is the work of grieving collectively. Of honoring loss while also affirming life. Of acknowledging pain while also claiming joy. Of carrying the past while also creating the future.

We are not broken.
We are remembering.
And in remembering, we are healing.

CHAPTER 7

THE BODY REMEMBERS

There were days when my body knew I was grieving before my mind could admit it. I would wake up tired, even after rest. My shoulders and my neck stayed tense. My breath felt shallow. I did not yet have language for what was happening, but my body was already holding the truth.

The exhaustion was pervasive, settling into my bones in a way that sleep could not fix. I would go to bed early, sleep through the night, and still wake feeling as if I had not rested at all. As if my body had been working all night, processing what my conscious mind refused to acknowledge during the day.

My shoulders carried a weight I could not name. The tension crept up toward my ears without my noticing, creating a pain that radiated down my back and up into my neck. I would catch myself mid-day, realize my shoulders were nearly touching my ears, and consciously lower them. But within minutes, they would creep back up. My body holding itself in a perpetual brace position, as if preparing for impact.

My breath was shallow, trapped in the upper part of my chest, never quite reaching deep into my lungs. I was breathing enough to survive but not enough to thrive, taking quick, shallow breaths that kept me in a constant state of low-level stress. I did not realize how shallow my breathing had become until I paid attention and noticed that I had not taken a full, deep breath in weeks, maybe months.

I did not yet have language for what was happening. I could not have told you that I was experiencing somatic grief, that my body was carrying what my mind was trying to avoid. I only knew that something felt wrong, that I was not okay, even if I could not articulate why.

But my body was already holding the truth. It knew what I was not ready to admit. That I was grieving. That the loss had affected me more deeply than I wanted to acknowledge. That no amount of pushing through or staying busy or pretending to be fine could change the fact that I was in pain.

Grief does not live only in our thoughts. It settles into our muscles, our nervous systems, our hearts. Long after the mind tries to move on, the body continues to carry what was never released. Science now confirms what so many of us have felt, our bodies store stress, trauma, and loss.

We think of grief as an emotional experience, something that happens in our minds and hearts. We talk about feeling sad, about missing someone, about the ache of absence. And all of that is true. But grief is also fundamentally physical. It is a full-body experience that shows up in ways we might not immediately recognize as grief.

It settles into our muscles as chronic tension. The shoulders that never quite relax. The jaw that clenches during sleep. The lower back that aches for no apparent reason. The neck that stays stiff and sore. These are not random pains. They are the body's response to carrying unprocessed emotion, to holding grief that has nowhere else to go.

Muscles tighten to protect us, to brace against pain, to create armor around vulnerable places. But when that tension becomes chronic, when muscles stay contracted day after day, they begin to hurt. They develop trigger points, knots that radiate pain to other areas. They restrict movement and limit flexibility. They become a source of ongoing discomfort that we might attribute to aging or poor posture when really, they are holding our grief.

It settles into our nervous systems as dysregulation. The sympathetic nervous system, responsible for the fight-or-flight response, becomes overactive. We exist in a state of hypervigilance, always scanning for threats, always on edge, never quite able to relax. Our heart rate stays elevated. Our blood pressure rises. Our bodies are constantly preparing for danger even when there is no immediate threat.

The parasympathetic nervous system, responsible for rest and recovery, struggles to engage. We cannot shift into a state of calm and safety. Even when we try to relax, even when we create space for rest, our nervous system stays activated. We lie in bed but cannot fall asleep. We sit down to relax but feel restless. Our bodies have forgotten how to truly rest.

This dysregulation affects everything. It impacts our sleep, our digestion, our immune function, our ability to concentrate. It creates a baseline state of stress that we learn to live with, that becomes so familiar we stop noticing it is there. Until we do notice, until we realize how exhausted we are, how on edge we have been, how long we have been living in survival mode.

It settles into our hearts, literally. The cardiovascular system responds to grief and stress with increased inflammation, elevated blood pressure, higher risk of heart disease. The phrase "broken heart syndrome" is not just poetic language. It is a real medical condition where intense emotional stress can cause heart muscle failure. Grief can literally affect the heart's ability to function.

Long after the mind tries to move on, the body continues to carry what was never released. We tell ourselves we are over it, that we have processed it, that we have moved on with our lives. But our bodies tell a different story. They hold the grief we never fully felt, the tears we never cried, the rage we never expressed, the fear we never acknowledged.

Science now confirms what so many of us have felt. The field of psychoneuroimmunology studies how psychological stress affects the nervous system and immune function. Research shows that unprocessed trauma and grief can lead to chronic inflammation, weakened immune response, increased susceptibility to illness. Our bodies quite literally store stress, trauma, and loss at a cellular level.

Studies using brain imaging show that emotional pain activates the same neural pathways as physical pain. The brain does not distinguish between the two. Grief hurts, not metaphorically but actually. It creates real, measurable changes in the body, in brain chemistry, in stress hormones, in immune markers.

The ACE (Adverse Childhood Experiences) study demonstrated that early trauma has long-term health consequences. Adults who experienced trauma in childhood have higher rates of heart disease, diabetes, cancer, and autoimmune conditions. The trauma lives in their bodies decades later, affecting their physical health in profound ways.

For Black communities, this embodied grief is often layered with years of survival. We learn to push through exhaustion, to ignore discomfort, to keep going no matter the cost. Over time, this endurance becomes our default, even when our bodies are asking us to slow down.

The historical context matters. Our ancestors had to push through physical discomfort to survive. They could not afford to rest when they were tired, to heal when they were sick, to slow down when they were in pain. Survival meant continuing to work, continuing to function, continuing to move forward regardless of what their bodies needed.

This capacity for endurance was adaptive. It kept people alive. It allowed them to survive conditions that should have killed them. And it was passed down through generations, both through taught behavior and through epigenetic changes, as a survival mechanism.

But what was adaptive in contexts of enslavement and ongoing oppression can become maladaptive when applied indiscriminately. When we push through exhaustion that is our body's signal to rest. When we ignore pain that is our body's signal that something is wrong. When we override our body's wisdom in service of productivity, of not being seen as weak, of meeting external expectations.

We learn to push through exhaustion because rest has historically been a luxury we could not afford. Because taking time off meant losing income we desperately needed. Because showing weakness meant being vulnerable in contexts where vulnerability was dangerous. Because strength has been our armor and letting that armor down felt too risky.

We learn to ignore discomfort because pain is so common, so pervasive, that we begin to see it as normal. We do not question why we always have headaches, why our stomachs are always upset, why we are always sore. We assume this is just how bodies feel, especially as we age, especially given the stress we are under.

We learn to keep going no matter the cost because stopping feels impossible. Because we have responsibilities, people depending on us, work that cannot wait. Because we have been taught that our worth is tied to our productivity, that we earn our place by what we contribute, that rest is something to be earned rather than something we inherently deserve.

Over time, this endurance becomes our default. We no longer consciously choose to push through. We do it automatically, without thinking, because it is the pattern we have learned. Even when our bodies are asking us to slow down, sending us clear signals through pain, through fatigue, through illness, we override those signals and keep moving.

Even when our bodies are asking us to slow down. Through the persistent headache that will not go away. Through the digestive issues that flare up during stress. Through the chronic pain that limits our movement. Through the exhaustion that no amount of sleep seems to fix. Through the colds and infections that happen more frequently because our immune system is worn down.

These are not random symptoms. They are our bodies speaking, trying to get our attention, trying to tell us that something needs to change. But we have been trained not to listen. We have been taught to medicate the symptoms and keep moving, to push through the pain, to view our bodies as machines that should keep running regardless of maintenance needs.

When grief remains unprocessed, it finds its way into our physical health, headaches, chronic pain, digestive issues, fatigue, and anxiety. We may seek medical explanations, never realizing that our bodies are speaking the language of loss.

The headaches that come and go without clear trigger. The migraines that lay us out for days at a time. The tension headaches that sit at the base of the skull or wrap around like a band. These can be expressions of grief held in the body, of stress that has nowhere else to go, of emotions that are locked in muscles and nerves.

The chronic pain that doctors cannot fully explain. The fibromyalgia, the unexplained joint pain, the back problems that imaging does not account for. Pain that is real, that affects quality of life significantly, but that does not have a clear structural cause. This can be somatic pain, the body expressing through physical sensation what cannot be expressed emotionally.

The digestive issues that flare during times of stress. The irritable bowel syndrome, the acid reflux, the nausea, the stomach pain. The gut is deeply connected to the nervous system, often called the "second brain." When we are stressed or grieving, our digestion is affected. The gut holds emotion, holds trauma, responds to what we feel even when we are not consciously aware of feeling it.

The fatigue that is more than just tiredness. The exhaustion that makes getting out of bed feel like climbing a mountain. The lack of energy that makes even simple tasks feel overwhelming. This can be depression, yes, but it can also be the body's response to carrying too much for too long, to never fully resting, to using all available resources just to get through each day.

The anxiety that seems to come from nowhere. The racing heart, the difficulty breathing, the sense of impending doom. Anxiety is often grief in disguise, the body's response to unprocessed loss, to carrying pain that has not been acknowledged, to the stress of pretending everything is fine when it is not.

We seek medical explanations for these symptoms. We go to doctors, get tests run, try medications. And sometimes there are medical issues that need treatment. But often, the root cause is not purely physical. It is emotional and spiritual pain being expressed through the body. It is grief that has been suppressed manifesting as physical symptoms.

Never realizing that our bodies are speaking the language of loss. That the pain is communication, that the fatigue is information, that the illness is invitation. Invitation to slow down, to pay attention, to acknowledge what we have been avoiding. Our bodies are trying to tell us something. The question is whether we are willing to listen.

Healing invites us to listen. To notice where tension lives. To honor what our bodies are holding. Rest is not weakness, it is wisdom. The body remembers, but it can also release.

Listening to the body requires slowing down enough to actually feel what is there. In our fast-paced, productivity-obsessed culture, this is countercultural. We are taught to ignore body signals, to override discomfort, to keep moving. Listening requires something different. It requires pausing. It requires tuning in.

It might mean doing a body scan, slowly bringing attention to each part of the body and noticing what is there. Where is there tension? Where is there pain? Where does the body feel open and where does it feel closed? This is not about judging or fixing. It is simply about noticing.

It might mean paying attention to patterns. When does the headache come? What happens before the stomach pain starts? What emotions were present before the body tightened up? Our bodies have wisdom. They respond to emotional states, to environmental stressors, to unmet needs. Learning to read those responses helps us understand what we need.

To notice where tension lives. Not just in the moment but chronically. Where do you always hold tension? Is it your shoulders, your jaw, your lower back, your hips? These places of chronic tension are often places where emotion is stored, where trauma is held, where grief has settled in.

Noticing is the first step. Once we notice where tension lives, we can begin to work with it. Through gentle movement, through massage, through therapy that addresses somatic experience, through practices like yoga or tai chi that combine movement with awareness. Through simply breathing into those places, bringing attention and warmth and permission to soften.

To honor what our bodies are holding. This means acknowledging that the body is not just carrying us around. It is holding our experiences, our emotions, our history. It deserves to be treated with respect, with care, with gratitude. It has been working hard to keep us alive, to help us survive, to carry us through.

Honoring might mean thanking the body for what it does. Thanking the heart for beating, the lungs for breathing, the legs for carrying us, the hands for their work. It might mean apologizing to the body for times we pushed too hard, ignored its signals, treated it harshly. It might mean making commitments to care for it better going forward.

Rest is not weakness, it is wisdom. This is a radical statement in communities where rest has been coded as laziness, where pushing through is valorized, where worth is tied to productivity. But rest is essential for healing. The body repairs during rest. The nervous system resets. The immune system strengthens. Emotions process. Grief moves.

Rest looks different for different people. For some, it is sleep. For others, it is quiet time alone. For some, it is being in nature. For others, it is engaging in gentle, pleasurable activities that do not demand anything. The key is that it is restorative, that it fills rather than depletes, that it gives the body permission to soften and release.

The body remembers, but it can also release. This is the hope. Yes, our bodies hold trauma and grief. Yes, they carry what has not been processed. Yes, they store stress at a cellular level. But they also have the capacity to heal, to release, to transform.

Release happens through many pathways. Through crying, which actually changes the chemical composition of our tears and releases stress hormones. Through shaking and trembling, the body's natural response to discharge activation after threat. Through deep breathing, which signals safety to the nervous system. Through movement, which helps process emotion that is stuck.

Release happens through somatic therapies that work directly with the body. EMDR (Eye Movement Desensitization and Reprocessing), which helps process traumatic memories. Somatic Experiencing, which focuses on body sensations and the completion of self-protective responses. Trauma-informed yoga, which creates space for gentle movement and awareness in a safe container.

Release happens through touch, when it is safe and consensual. Massage that helps muscles finally let go. Human touch, when it is nurturing and non-demanding, can communicate safety to a nervous system that has been on high alert.

Release happens through creative expression. Dance that lets the body move grief. Drumming that gives rhythm to emotion. Singing that opens the throat and chest. Art that externalizes what is internal. These practices engage the body in ways that talk therapy cannot, accessing what is held beneath language.

The body remembers. It holds our history, our grief, our trauma. But it also holds our resilience, our capacity for healing, our innate wisdom. When we learn to listen to it, to honor what it holds, to give it space to release what it no longer needs to carry, profound healing becomes possible.

This is not quick work. Bodies that have been holding grief for years, for decades, for generations, need time to release. They need patience, gentleness, consistent care. But it is possible. The body wants to heal. It is designed for resilience. When given the right conditions, space, safety, support, it knows what to do.

And as the body releases, as tension softens and breath deepens and the nervous system settles, we often find that emotional healing follows. That the grief we could not feel when it was locked in the body becomes accessible. That the tears we could not cry finally come. That the anger we could not express finds voice. That the pain we could not acknowledge becomes something we can hold, can witness, can eventually let go of.

The body remembers. But it also teaches us. About what we need. About what we have survived. About our capacity for both holding and releasing. About the wisdom of slowing down, of listening, of honoring the truth that lives in our bones.

This is embodied healing. Not just healing the mind or the spirit but healing the whole self. Recognizing that we are integrated beings, that what affects one part affects all parts, that true healing must include the body.

Our bodies have carried us through so much. They deserve our attention, our care, our gratitude. They deserve rest. They deserve to be heard. They deserve to release what they no longer need to hold.

And when we give them that, when we honor the body's wisdom and work with it rather than against it, we open pathways to healing that cognitive approaches alone cannot reach. We access grief at its deepest level and create space for it to move, to transform, to integrate.

The body remembers. And in remembering, in releasing, in healing, it teaches us how to be whole again.

CHAPTER 8

WHEN THERAPY DOESN'T FEEL SAFE

For many Black individuals, therapy has not always felt like a place of refuge. Too often, it has been a place of misunderstanding, where our pain is viewed through a lens that does not see our full humanity.

The therapeutic relationship is built on trust. It requires vulnerability, the willingness to share the most tender, wounded parts of ourselves with another person. But trust is not given freely. It must be earned. And for Black people, who have repeatedly experienced betrayal from institutions that claimed to help, trust in therapeutic spaces cannot be assumed.

Too often, therapy has been a place where our experiences are questioned. Where the reality of racism is treated as perception rather than fact. Where our responses to discrimination are pathologized rather than understood as normal reactions to abnormal circumstances. Where our cultural expressions are viewed as symptoms rather than strengths.

Too often, therapy has been a place where we have had to educate rather than be supported. Where we spend our sessions explaining microaggressions to therapists who do not recognize them. Where we have to justify why a particular interaction was racist before we can discuss how it affected us. Where we translate our experiences into language that makes sense within dominant frameworks instead of having our experiences understood on their own terms.

Too often, therapy has been a place where our pain is minimized. Where grief that should be acknowledged is instead redirected. Where trauma is individualized when it is collective. Where the ongoing nature of our suffering is not recognized because therapists are trained to look for discrete events rather than chronic conditions.

Our pain is viewed through a lens that does not see our full humanity. Through a lens shaped by stereotypes about Black people, about who we are and how we should behave. Through a lens that sees strength as our defining characteristic and therefore questions our vulnerability. Through a lens that assumes dysfunction where there is adaptation. Through a lens that does not account for the reality that we are navigating a world that was not designed for our wellbeing.

This lens is not neutral. It is shaped by the same racist ideology that permeates other systems. And when it is applied in therapeutic spaces, it causes harm. It retraumatizes people who came seeking healing. It reinforces the very dynamics that caused the pain in the first place.

We carry a history of systems that have not protected us, and that history shows up when we consider asking for help. Fear of being judged, misdiagnosed, or dismissed can make vulnerability feel risky. Sometimes, it is safer to remain silent than to be misunderstood.

The history of mental health systems and Black communities is marked by harm. From the use of psychiatric diagnoses to justify slavery and segregation, to the forced sterilization of Black women deemed "unfit," to the overdiagnosis of schizophrenia in Black men during the civil rights movement, to the ongoing disparities in how Black people are diagnosed and treated, this history creates legitimate wariness.

Mental health systems have been tools of social control. They have been used to pathologize resistance, to label normal responses to oppression as mental illness, to justify confinement and medication as solutions to problems that were social and political. This is not ancient history. This continues in how Black children are more likely to be diagnosed with conduct disorders while white children with similar behaviors are diagnosed with ADHD. In how Black adults are more likely to be involuntarily committed, more likely to be prescribed antipsychotic medications, and less likely to receive psychotherapy.

This history shows up in the present. It creates hesitation. When you know that people who look like you have been harmed by systems claiming to help, when you know that your expressions of pain might be misinterpreted, when you know that asking for help might result in more harm than healing, the logical response is caution.

Fear of being judged is real. Black people often feel that they are representing their entire race in interactions with non-Black people, that their individual behavior will be generalized. In therapy, this can mean feeling pressure to present as together, as strong, as coping well, because showing struggle might reinforce negative stereotypes. It can mean hiding parts of yourself, moderating your expressions, being strategic about what you share.

Fear of being misdiagnosed is grounded in reality. Studies show that Black people are more likely to be diagnosed with more severe mental illnesses than white people presenting with the same symptoms. That cultural expressions of distress, ways of describing experiences that make sense within Black communities, are sometimes interpreted as psychosis. That valid anger about discrimination is labeled as pathology. That normal grief is diagnosed as depression requiring medication.

Fear of being dismissed is based on lived experience. Of having therapists minimize your concerns, redirect conversations away from racism, suggest that you are being too sensitive or reading too much into situations. Of being told to focus on what you can control, as if the problem is your reaction rather than the systems causing harm. Of leaving sessions feeling more alone than when you arrived because your reality was not validated.

Sometimes, it is safer to remain silent than to be misunderstood. Silence protects. It keeps your pain private, where it cannot be misinterpreted or used against you. It allows you to maintain control over your narrative. It prevents the additional harm that can come from having your experiences questioned or minimized.

But silence also isolates. It means carrying burdens alone. It means not receiving the support that could help. It means that the harm continues unchallenged, that the systems that need to change remain unchanged because the pain they cause stays hidden.

This is the impossible choice many Black people face. Risk vulnerability in spaces that may not be safe or protect yourself through silence and miss out on potential healing. Neither option is good. Both carry costs.

Microaggressions, cultural assumptions, and lack of representation create barriers that are rarely discussed but deeply felt. When we must explain our culture before we can explain our pain, the burden becomes too heavy.

Microaggressions in therapy can be subtle. A therapist who consistently mispronounces your name and does not correct themselves. Comments about how "articulate" you are. Surprise when you mention your education or professional achievements. Assumptions about your family structure, your religious background, your experiences. These may seem small, but they accumulate. They communicate that you are not fully seen, that the therapist holds biases they have not examined.

Microaggressions can be more overt. Questioning whether racism really played a role in an experience you are describing. Suggesting that if you just changed your behavior or attitude, you would not experience discrimination. Asking you to educate them about Black culture, about hair, about code-switching, about things they should have learned in their training. Treating you as a representative of all Black people rather than as an individual.

Each microaggression is a small cut. And therapy is supposed to be a place of healing, not a place where you accumulate more wounds. When you are paying for a service, when you are making yourself vulnerable, when you are coming for help with pain you are already carrying, you should not also have to manage your therapist's biases.

Cultural assumptions create distance. When therapists assume that all families function the same way, that all expressions of emotion mean the same thing, that all spiritual beliefs fit within Christian frameworks, that all forms of healing look like Western psychology, they miss important aspects of their clients' experiences.

Black culture is not monolithic. There is tremendous diversity within Black communities, across geography, class, nationality, generation, religion, sexuality. But there are also shared experiences, shared values, shared ways of understanding the world that are shaped by the experience of Blackness in a racist society. Therapists who do not understand this, who apply universal frameworks without accounting for cultural context, miss critical information.

The assumption that individual therapy is the gold standard ignores the collectivist orientation of many Black communities, where healing happens in relationship, where community is central to identity. The assumption that verbal processing is the primary path to healing does not account for other forms of expression, spiritual practices, movement, creativity. The assumption that the goal is individual happiness misses the reality that for many Black people, the goal is collective liberation, and individual healing is inextricably linked to community wellbeing.

Lack of representation compounds these issues. When the overwhelming majority of therapists are white, when Black therapists are rare and in high demand, when finding a therapist who shares your cultural background feels impossible, representation itself becomes a barrier. Not because only Black therapists can help Black clients, but because the lack of diversity in the field signals that Black experiences are not centered, that Black voices are not shaping the profession, that the systems of care were not built with Black people in mind.

When we must explain our culture before we can explain our pain, the burden becomes too heavy. Therapy should be a place where you can focus on your own healing. Where the therapist has done their homework, has educated themselves, has examined their biases. Where you do not have to teach them about racism before you can discuss how racism has affected you. Where your cultural practices are understood or at least approached with genuine curiosity and respect rather than judgment.

But too often, Black clients find themselves in the position of educator. Explaining why a particular comment was hurtful. Describing what it means to be Black in predominantly white spaces. Teaching therapists about stereotypes they should already recognize. This is exhausting. It takes energy away from the actual work of therapy. It positions the client as responsible for the therapist's learning rather than the other way around.

And after a while, it becomes too much. The burden of having to explain everything, to translate your experience, to manage your therapist's discomfort, to correct their assumptions, becomes heavier than the burden of carrying your pain alone. And so people drop out of therapy, not because they do not need help but because the help available requires too much additional labor.

True healing spaces must feel safe, affirming, and respectful. They must allow us to be whole, cultural, spiritual, emotional beings. Therapy should not ask us to leave parts of ourselves at the door.

Safety in therapy means more than physical safety. It means emotional safety, the sense that you will not be judged, that your experiences will be believed, that your pain will be taken seriously. It means cultural safety, the confidence that your identity will be respected, that your cultural practices will be honored, that you will not face discrimination in this space.

Safety is created through therapist competence. Through training in cultural humility, in racial trauma, in the specific ways that racism affects mental health. Through therapists doing their own work around bias and privilege. Through ongoing education and supervision. Through accountability when harm is caused.

Safety is communicated through explicit statements. Through therapists naming their awareness of power dynamics, acknowledging the history of harm in mental health systems, inviting feedback about the therapeutic relationship. Through creating explicit norms about confidentiality, about what will and will not be pathologized, about how cultural differences will be navigated.

Safety is built through consistency. Through therapists showing up reliably, following through on commitments, maintaining appropriate boundaries. Through predictability in a world that is often unpredictable and unsafe for Black people. Through creating a container that holds without constraining.

Affirming means actively validating the client's experiences and identity. Not just being neutral about race but actively affirming Blackness, recognizing the beauty and strength in Black culture, understanding racism as real and pervasive. Not just tolerating differences but celebrating them. Not just allowing clients to bring their whole selves but actively inviting it.

Affirmation looks like incorporating cultural strengths into treatment. Recognizing the role of spirituality and faith for many Black clients. Valuing community and family connections rather than pathologizing interdependence. Understanding that resistance to oppression is healthy, that self-protection is adaptive, that strategies that might look like avoidance or anger in one framework are wise responses in the context of ongoing threat.

Respectful means treating Black clients with the same dignity afforded to all clients but also understanding that respect requires cultural competence. It means asking about preferences rather than assuming. It means being willing to be corrected. It means acknowledging when you do not know something rather than pretending expertise you do not have.

Respect means recognizing that the client is the expert on their own experience. That however they describe their pain is valid. That their interpretation of events is legitimate even if it differs from the therapist's initial understanding. That they have survived this far for good reasons and that any coping strategies they have developed make sense given what they have endured.

They must allow us to be whole, cultural, spiritual, emotional beings. Therapy should not ask us to leave parts of ourselves at the door. We cannot be asked to separate our racial identity from our mental health, our cultural context from our individual experience, our spirituality from our healing. These are integrated. They are part of who we are.

Whole-person therapy recognizes that humans are complex, multifaceted, shaped by multiple intersecting identities and experiences. That you cannot address depression without also addressing the racism that contributes to it. That you cannot treat anxiety without acknowledging the legitimate reasons Black people have to feel unsafe. That you cannot support healing without honoring all the sources of strength clients draw from, including faith, community, cultural traditions.

When therapy allows for wholeness, when it does not require compartmentalization, when it honors the full humanity of Black clients, it becomes a place of genuine healing. Not perfect, because therapy is a human endeavor and humans are flawed. But real, because it is built on a foundation of respect, understanding, and authentic connection.

We deserve care that understands us. We deserve spaces that honor our stories.

This is not asking for special treatment. This is asking for competent treatment. For care that is informed by an understanding of the specific ways that racism affects mental health. For therapists who have done the work to examine their own biases. For systems that recognize the barriers Black people face in accessing care and work to remove those barriers.

We deserve care that understands us. Care that does not require us to translate our experiences into frameworks that do not fit. Care that recognizes the legitimacy of our pain without questioning whether it is real. Care that sees our coping strategies as adaptive rather than dysfunctional. Care that addresses both the individual and the systemic factors affecting our wellbeing.

We deserve therapists who understand that racism is trauma. Who recognize that the stress of navigating predominantly white spaces, of experiencing microaggressions daily, of carrying the weight of representation, of worrying about safety in ways that white people do not have to worry, is real and significant. Who can hold space for both individual healing and collective grief.

We deserve access to therapists who share our cultural background when that is what we prefer. Not because non-Black therapists cannot help Black clients, but because there is something powerful about being seen by someone who inherently understands aspects of your experience. Who does not need everything explained. Who gets the cultural references. Who shares the cultural knowledge. And the fact that Black therapists are so few, so overextended, so hard to access, is a systemic problem that needs addressing.

We deserve spaces that honor our stories. That recognize that our narratives are not just individual tales of suffering but are connected to larger histories, larger communities, larger struggles for justice and dignity. That our stories carry wisdom, resistance, survival. That they deserve to be witnessed with reverence, not analyzed with pathology.

We deserve spaces where our healing is not just about symptom reduction but about reclaiming our full humanity. Where the goal is not just to help us function better in oppressive systems but to support our resistance to those systems. Where therapy is understood as part of liberation work, not separate from it.

This is what healing spaces should offer. Not perfection. Not the absence of all discomfort. Not the guarantee that therapy will always feel easy or safe. But the genuine effort to create conditions for healing. The humility to acknowledge when harm has been done. The commitment to do better.

When therapy is done well, when it is culturally informed and trauma-responsive and genuinely affirming, it can be transformative. It can provide the support that helps people not just survive but thrive. It can be part of individual healing and collective resistance.

But when therapy falls short, when it replicates the very dynamics that caused harm in the first place, it becomes another site of trauma. Another system that fails Black people. Another place where we learn that we cannot trust institutions to care for us.

We deserve better. We deserve care that sees us fully, honors us completely, supports us effectively. We deserve healing spaces that are safe. And until those spaces are widely available, until the mental health field does the work to become truly competent in serving Black communities, we will continue to seek healing in other places. In our communities. In our spiritual practices. In our creative expressions. In our resistance.

We will continue to heal ourselves and each other. Not because we should have to. But because we have always had to. Because our survival has always depended on it. Because we carry within us the wisdom of ancestors who healed despite everything. Because healing is our birthright, even when the systems meant to support it fail us.

And we will continue to demand better. To push for change in mental health systems. To train more Black therapists. To educate all therapists in cultural competence. To create new models of healing that center our experiences. To build spaces that serve us.

Because we deserve care that understands us. We deserve spaces that honor our stories. And we will not settle for less.

Chapter 9:

Telling Our Stories Out Loud

There is power in naming what has been hidden. When we tell our stories, we reclaim what grief tried to take, our voice, our identity, our truth.

For too long, grief has been kept private. Hidden behind closed doors, whispered in quiet moments, carried alone in the dark. We learned that our pain was not for public consumption, that vulnerability was weakness, that speaking our sorrow would burden others or reveal too much about our struggles.

But silence has a cost. It isolates us. It convinces us that our experiences are unique, that no one else could possibly understand, that we are alone in our suffering. It allows grief to grow unchecked, to become larger and more overwhelming because it has no witness, no container, no community to hold it.

Naming breaks that isolation. When we put words to what we have experienced, when we say out loud "this happened to me" or "this is how I feel" or "this is what I lost," we begin to shift our relationship with the pain. It is no longer an unnamed presence haunting us. It is something we can point to, something we can describe, something we can begin to work with.

Naming is an act of power. It asserts our right to define our own experience. To say what matters and what hurts. To claim space for our pain in a world that often wants to minimize or dismiss it. To refuse the silence that has been imposed on us or that we have imposed on ourselves.

When we tell our stories, we reclaim what grief tried to take. Grief can strip us of so much. It takes the person or the dream or the future we were counting on. But it can also take our sense of self, our confidence in our own perceptions, our ability to trust that what we feel is real and valid.

Telling our stories returns these things to us. It says, "my grief matters." It says, "my experience is legitimate." It says, "I have a right to name what has been lost and to express how it has affected me." It reclaims voice in spaces where we have been silenced. It reclaims identity when grief has made us feel like we no longer know who we are. It reclaims truth in the face of narratives that would minimize or distort our experiences.

Our voice is powerful. It has been used throughout history as a tool of resistance, a way of asserting humanity in contexts that denied it. From slave narratives to civil rights testimonies to Black Lives Matter activism, Black voices speaking truth have been essential to survival and liberation. When we speak our grief, we stand in that tradition. We use our voices to claim space, to demand recognition, to insist that our pain counts.

Our identity is complex and multifaceted, but grief can make us feel flattened, reduced to our loss, defined by our pain. Telling our stories allows us to be whole again. To say yes, I am grieving, and I am also all these other things. I am a mother, a sister, a friend, a professional, a creative, a spiritual being. My grief is part of my story, but it is not the whole story.

Our truth is ours to tell. Not the sanitized version that makes others comfortable. Not the compressed version that fits into acceptable timeframes. Not the version that minimizes the impact or rushes to resolution. But the messy, complicated, ongoing truth of what we have experienced and how we are navigating it.

Silence may have once protected us, but it no longer serves us. Speaking does not erase pain, but it allows it to move. It reminds us that we are not alone and that our experiences matter.

There were times when silence was necessary. When speaking about pain could bring more harm. When vulnerability was dangerous. When the only way to survive was to keep your grief private and your face neutral. Our ancestors knew this. They carried their pain in silence because the alternative was worse.

But we are not in the same circumstances. We have different options available. And while speaking is still not without risk, while there are still contexts where vulnerability can be weaponized, there are also spaces where it can be honored. Where our stories can be received with care. Where speaking truth creates connection rather than isolation.

Silence no longer serves us when it keeps us separated from the very support we need. When it prevents us from accessing resources that could help. When it allows pain to fester unchecked. When it makes us believe we are alone in experiences that are actually shared.

Speaking does not erase pain. This is important to acknowledge. Telling our stories is not a cure. It does not make grief disappear. It does not undo the loss or eliminate the hurt. Anyone who suggests that simply talking about it will fix it is oversimplifying the reality of grief.

But speaking allows pain to move. When grief is held in silence, it becomes stuck. It circles endlessly in our minds, the same thoughts repeating, the same emotions churning with no outlet. It builds pressure with nowhere to release. It becomes stagnant, heavy, immovable.

When we speak it, something shifts. The pain moves from internal to external. It takes shape in words. It enters the space between us and another person. It becomes something that can be witnessed, held, responded to. It is no longer trapped inside us, and in that movement, even if the pain itself has not diminished, our relationship to it changes.

Speaking allows us to hear ourselves. Sometimes we do not fully know what we think or feel until we say it out loud. The act of putting experience into language clarifies it, reveals aspects we had not consciously recognized, helps us understand our own reactions better.

Speaking allows others to witness. And there is something profound about being seen in our pain, about having another person acknowledge what we have endured and validate that it matters. Witness does not fix or solve, but it does make the burden lighter because we are no longer carrying it entirely alone.

It reminds us that we are not alone. This is perhaps one of the most powerful aspects of storytelling. When we speak our truth and others say, "me too" or "I understand" or "something similar happened to me," we realize that our experience, while unique in its details, is not singular. That others have walked similar paths. That the feelings we thought were ours alone are shared.

This realization is healing. Not because it makes our pain less real, but because it makes us less isolated in it. Because it creates community where there was loneliness. Because it reminds us that we are part of a larger human experience, connected to others through our shared vulnerability.

And it reminds us that our experiences matter. In a world that often tells Black people that our pain does not count, that our losses are less important, that our grief should be brief and quiet, speaking our stories is an act of resistance. It asserts that we matter. That what happened to us matters. That our feelings about it are legitimate and deserving of attention.

Stories connect us. They create bridges where isolation once lived. They transform private pain into shared understanding. When one person speaks, others find permission to follow.

Human beings are storytelling creatures. We make sense of our experiences through narrative. We understand ourselves and each other through the stories we tell. And stories have a unique power to create connection across difference, to help us understand experiences we have not personally lived, to build empathy and solidarity.

When someone shares their grief story, they are offering a piece of themselves. They are saying, "this is what I have lived through, this is how it has affected me, this is what I need you to know." And when we listen, really listen, we receive that offering. We honor it. We allow it to expand our understanding of what grief can look like, how it can show up, what it can require.

Stories create bridges where isolation once lived. Before the story is told, each person exists in their own private world of pain, unaware that others are experiencing something similar. The story becomes the bridge that connects those separate experiences, that allows people to find each other, to recognize shared ground, to realize they are not alone.

This is especially powerful in communities where certain losses or certain expressions of grief have been stigmatized or silenced. When someone breaks that silence, when they tell the story that has been kept hidden, they create a pathway for others. They make it safer for the next person to speak. They begin to normalize what had been treated as shameful or abnormal.

Stories transform private pain into shared understanding. What was once locked inside one person's experience becomes available to a wider community. Others can witness it, learn from it, be changed by it. The pain itself may not change, but its meaning can shift when it is shared. It can become not just personal suffering but also collective knowledge. Not just individual loss but also communal grief that the community can hold together.

This transformation does not minimize the individual's pain. It honors it by recognizing its significance, by allowing it to matter not just to the person who experienced it but to others as well. It says that this pain has meaning beyond its personal impact, that it teaches us something, connects us to something larger, contributes to our collective understanding.

When one person speaks, others find permission to follow. This is how movements begin. One voice breaks the silence. That voice gives courage to another. And another. And soon what was once unspeakable becomes speakable. What was once hidden becomes visible. What was once shameful becomes acknowledged as part of the shared human experience.

We see this pattern in many contexts. #MeToo began with individuals sharing their stories of sexual harassment and assault, giving others permission to say "this happened to me too." Black Lives Matter gained momentum as people shared stories of police violence and racial injustice. Every social movement toward recognition and change has been powered by individuals willing to speak their truth and others willing to listen and add their voices.

The same dynamic happens with grief. When one person shares how they are struggling with a particular kind of loss, others who have experienced similar losses feel permission to name their own struggles. When someone speaks about the ongoing nature of their grief, refusing the narrative that they should be "over it" by now, others feel freed from that same expectation. When someone names the cultural factors that affect their grieving, others recognize those factors in their own experience.

Permission is powerful. We often do not realize how much we are waiting for permission, for some signal that it is okay to feel what we feel or say what we think. And when someone else goes first, when they model vulnerability and honesty, they grant that permission. Not explicitly, not formally, but through the simple act of being brave enough to speak.

Healing begins when we are heard.
And we are worthy of being heard.

Healing is not a solo journey. While there is important internal work that each person must do, healing also requires connection. It requires being seen, being known, being held in our pain by others who can witness without trying to fix, who can sit with our sorrow without needing to make it go away.

Being heard is different from being listened to. Listening is the technical act of receiving sound. Hearing is deeper. It is receiving the meaning, the emotion, the humanity behind the words. It is understanding not just what is being said but what it costs to say it. It is honoring the trust inherent in someone sharing their pain.

When we are heard, something in us relaxes. The part of us that has been holding so tightly, that has been afraid to let go because we thought no one would understand or care, can finally exhale. We are reminded that we are not alone. That our experience is real and valid. That we matter.

This is why representation matters in healing spaces. Why it is important to have people who understand our cultural context, our lived experiences, the specific ways that our identities shape our grief. Because being heard by someone who gets it, who does not need extensive explanation, who can hold the complexity of our experience without judgment, is profoundly healing.

This is why community is essential. Individual therapy, while valuable, is not sufficient. We need spaces where Black people can gather and share their stories with others who will understand in ways that people outside the community cannot. We need circles and groups and gatherings where our grief can be witnessed by those who know, viscerally, what we are talking about.

I have been in physical spaces that hold the collective pain and the collective healing of thousands of people, free of charge. Beautiful spaces. Sacred spaces. Spaces where people come broken and leave lighter. Where grief is held with reverence and tenderness. Where no one is turned away because they cannot pay.

And although they do not discriminate, although their doors are open to all, the majority of people who take advantage of the space and who are facilitators at the space do not look like us.

This is not a criticism of those spaces. They are doing important work. They are serving people who desperately need what they offer. But their existence also reveals a gap. A need that is not being met. A longing that remains unfulfilled.

We deserve spaces in our communities for our pain to be turned into healing. Spaces in our neighborhoods, accessible without long commutes or complicated transportation. Spaces where the faces we see reflected back at us are Black faces. Where the people holding space for our grief understand not just theoretically but experientially what it means to grieve while Black.

We deserve the assistance of people who look like us walking alongside us. Not because non-Black facilitators cannot help, but because there is something profoundly powerful about being held by someone who shares your lived experience. Who does not need you to explain the cultural context. Who gets it without you having to translate. Who knows in their bones what you are talking about when you describe a particular kind of pain.

These spaces should exist. They must exist. And we must create them if they do not. Because healing that is accessible, culturally grounded, and community-based is healing that can reach people who would never walk into a therapist's office. People who cannot afford traditional therapy. People who have been harmed by formal mental health systems. People who need community more than they need credentials.

Creating these spaces requires resources, yes. But it also requires commitment. A belief that Black grief matters enough to invest in. That our communities deserve healing spaces as beautiful and well-resourced as any that exist elsewhere. That we should not have to leave our neighborhoods or our cultural contexts to access quality grief support.

Healing begins when we are heard. Not when we are fixed or when our pain is taken away or when everything is made better. But when someone truly hears us, sees us, acknowledges us in our pain. That is where healing starts. In the connection that happens when we speak our truth, and it is received with care.

And we are worthy of being heard. This should not need to be said, but in a world that often treats Black pain as less important, it does need to be said. We are worthy. Our stories matter. Our grief deserves attention, care, witness, space.

We do not have to earn the right to be heard by making our pain palatable, by keeping it brief, by wrapping it in redemptive narratives. We do not have to minimize our suffering or rush to resolution. We do not have to perform strength or hide vulnerability.

We are worthy of being heard exactly as we are. In our mess, in our ongoing struggle, in our complicated emotions, in our cultural specificity. We are worthy of spaces that honor our stories without requiring us to translate or explain or justify. We are worthy of people who can hold our pain without needing to solve it.

This worthiness is inherent. It does not depend on how we grieve or how long we grieve or whether our grief fits expected patterns. It is ours simply because we are human, because we have experienced loss, because we carry pain that deserves acknowledgment.

Claiming this worthiness is itself an act of healing. It is rejecting the messages that tell us our pain does not matter. It is insisting on our own humanity. It is refusing to be silenced or minimized or dismissed. It is stepping into our power as storytellers, as witnesses to our own lives, as people whose experiences have value and meaning.

When we tell our stories out loud, we do more than share information. We create possibility. We build community. We challenge silence. We honor our grief and the grief of those who came before us. We make space for those who will come after us to tell their stories too.

We reclaim our voices. We assert our right to be heard. We remind ourselves and each other that we are not alone, that our experiences matter, that our pain is real and worthy of witness.

This is the power of storytelling. Not that it erases pain, but that it transforms it. Not that it solves grief, but that it makes grief something we can hold together rather than carry alone. Not that it provides answers, but that it creates connection.

And in that connection, in that witness, in that shared understanding, healing becomes possible. Not healing that looks like forgetting or moving on, but healing that looks like integration, like being able to hold both the pain of what was lost and the fullness of who we are. Healing that honors the past while also making space for the present and future.

Our stories are powerful. They deserve to be told. And we deserve to be heard.

So we speak. We name what has been hidden. We break the silence. We tell our truth. We create bridges. We build community.

We heal, together, through the power of our voices raised in honest testimony about what we have survived and how we continue to carry it.

This is our work. This is our right. This is our healing.

CHAPTER 10

HOLDING SPACE IN BLACK COMMUNITIES

Before many of us ever step into a therapist's office, we learn how to grieve in community. We gather in kitchens after funerals. We sit in church pews surrounded by hymns and tears. We show up at repasts, in living rooms, on front porches, holding one another in ways that feel familiar and safe.

Community care is our first language of healing. Long before Western psychology offered its theories and therapies, Black communities developed their own practices for navigating loss. These practices were not formalized, not written in textbooks, not taught in universities. They were passed down through generations, learned by watching and participating, embedded in the rhythms of communal life.

We learn this language early. We learn it by observing how adults respond when someone dies. How neighbors appear at the door with food before they are asked. How church members organize themselves to ensure the bereaved family has what they need. How people simply show up, offering their presence as a form of support that requires no words.

We learn it through participation. By helping to prepare food for the repast. By sitting quietly with grieving relatives. By being part of the circle of care that surrounds loss. These experiences teach us that grief is not something to be handled alone, that community has a responsibility to the bereaved, that we hold each other through the hardest times.

We gather in kitchens after funerals. The kitchen becomes a hub of activity, a place where food is prepared and served, where people congregate naturally, where conversations flow. There is something about the kitchen that invites intimacy, that makes it easier to talk, to cry, to laugh, to be human together in all our complexity.

In these kitchen gatherings, healing happens through the ordinary acts of feeding and being fed. Through the aunties who insist you eat even when you have no appetite. Through the cousins who wash dishes while sharing memories. Through the collective work of caring for bodies in grief, ensuring that basic needs are met even when everything else feels impossible.

We sit in church pews surrounded by hymns and tears. The church has long been a central institution in Black communities, not just a place of worship but a gathering place, a source of social support, a location where community is built and maintained. When loss occurs, the church responds.

The homegoing service is its own form of healing. The songs that acknowledge both sorrow and hope. The testimonies that celebrate life even as they mourn death. The prayers that hold the community's collective grief and lift it up. The ritual structure that provides a container for emotions that might otherwise feel overwhelming.

In church pews, we learn that we can cry in public, that tears are not shameful, that expressing grief is acceptable within certain bounds. We learn the language of spiritual comfort, the scriptures and songs that have sustained generations. We learn that we are part of something larger than ourselves, that our individual grief is held by a community of faith.

We show up at repasts, in living rooms, on front porches, holding one another in ways that feel familiar and safe. The repast is more than a meal after a funeral. It is a ritual of remembrance and reconnection. It is where stories are told, where laughter emerges through tears, where the person who died is made present through memory.

After so many deaths back-to-back after my father died, the repast was something I would look forward to every time. The idea of looking forward to anything associated with death might sound strange to people outside the culture, but those who know, know.

You get to reunite with family and friends you have not seen for decades. Cousins who moved away. Childhood friends who went to different cities. Relatives who only show up for weddings and funerals, and lately it has been mostly funerals. You catch up on the latest gossip to distract you from your pain. Who is having a baby. Who got divorced. Who finally retired. Who started a business. The mundane details of living that feel like a lifeline when you are drowning in grief.

You get to wipe your tears for a minute and laugh and commune with your people. The same people who were crying with you in the church are now laughing in the fellowship hall, plates piled high with macaroni and cheese and collard greens. And this is not disrespectful. This is survival. This is how we hold both sorrow and joy. This is how we remember that even in the midst of death, life continues.

You get to see the children who have grown into teenagers. The last time you saw them they were in elementary school, and now they are taller than you, with voices that have changed and attitudes that make you laugh. You get to see the cool aunts whose hair is now gray, whose faces show the years but whose spirits are still bright. You make empty promises that you will stay in touch, that you will not wait for another funeral to see each other again. You exchange numbers. You say "let's get together soon." And you mean it in the moment, even though you both know that the only time you will probably see each other is at the next funeral.

But the promise matters anyway. The intention matters. The acknowledgment that we should not need death to bring us together matters. Even if we do not follow through, even if life gets busy and the months pass and another funeral comes before that coffee date ever happens, the desire to do better is real.

The repast holds all of this. The grief and the gossip. The tears and the laughter. The remembering of who we lost and the reconnecting with who we still have. The heaviness of death and the lightness of life happening side by side, on paper plates, in church fellowship halls and family living rooms.

In living rooms, we sit with those who mourn. Sometimes talking, sometimes in silence. Presence matters more than words. The willingness to simply be there, to witness grief without trying to minimize it, to stay when others might leave because the pain feels too heavy.

On front porches, conversations happen in the in-between spaces. Where it is easier to talk because you are not making direct eye contact, because you can look out at the world while you speak, because the openness of the space feels less confining than indoor conversations. Where wisdom is shared across generations, where young people learn from elders how to carry sorrow and still find joy.

These ways of holding one another feel familiar and safe because they are ours. They reflect our values, our aesthetics, our ways of being in the world. They do not require translation or explanation. They are culturally congruent, aligned with how we understand relationships and community and care.

In these spaces, healing often happens quietly. It happens through food, through laughter, through stories that remind us who we are. It happens when someone sits beside us without trying to fix anything. When presence becomes the medicine.

Healing in community is rarely loud or dramatic. It does not announce itself. It unfolds in small moments, in gentle gestures, in the accumulation of care over time. It is quiet because it does not need to be performed. It is offered freely, received gratefully, and its effects are subtle but profound.

It happens through food. Food is love made tangible. It is nourishment for bodies that grief has made forget to eat. It is the physical expression of care, the labor of preparation offered as gift. In Black communities, food is central to every gathering, every celebration, every moment of mourning. It is how we say "I care about you" when words fail.

The dishes that appear, collard greens and macaroni and cheese, fried chicken and cornbread, sweet potato pie and pound cake, are more than sustenance. They are tradition, connection to ancestors who cooked these same foods, comfort in familiar flavors. They are offered with the understanding that grief lives in the body and that feeding the body is part of caring for the whole person.

It happens through laughter. This surprises people who are not familiar with Black mourning practices. How can there be laughter at a time of loss? But laughter is not disrespectful. It is life affirming. It is a reminder that joy and sorrow can coexist, that we can honor the dead while also celebrating the living, that grief does not require us to be somber every moment.

Laughter at repasts often comes through storytelling, through remembering funny moments, through inside jokes that connect those who knew the deceased. This laughter is healing because it reminds us that the person who died was more than their death, that they brought joy and humor into the world, that we can remember them with smiles as well as tears.

It happens through stories that remind us of who we are. Stories about the person who died, yes, but also stories about the family, the community, the shared history. Stories that locate us in a larger narrative, that connect us to those who came before, that remind us of our resilience and our roots.

These stories serve multiple purposes. They keep the deceased present in memory. They teach younger generations about their heritage. They reinforce community bonds. They provide perspective, reminding us that we have survived loss before and will survive it again. They create meaning, turning individual death into part of a collective story of survival and continuity.

It happens when someone sits beside us without trying to fix anything. This is perhaps the most powerful form of support. Not the person who offers platitudes or tries to make the pain go away, but the person who is willing to simply be present with us in our grief. Who can tolerate the discomfort of witnessing pain without needing to solve it.

This kind of presence requires emotional maturity. It requires being comfortable with your own grief and pain so that you can sit with someone else's. It requires trusting that your presence matters even when you cannot make things better. It requires valuing being over doing, connection over solutions.

When presence becomes the medicine. Not advice or answers or attempts to cheer us up. Just presence. The quiet sitting with. The hand on the shoulder. The willingness to stay when everything in you wants to flee because grief is uncomfortable and scary and reminds you of your own losses and vulnerabilities.

Presence heals because it communicates worth. It says you matter enough for me to show up. Your pain is important enough for me to witness. You are not alone in this. And sometimes, that is exactly what we need. Not someone to take the pain away, but someone to affirm that we are not alone in carrying it.

Black communities have always known how to hold space, even when resources were scarce and pain was abundant. We learned to care for one another when systems failed us. We created rituals that honored loss and celebrated life at the same time.

This knowledge comes from necessity. When you are excluded from dominant institutions, when you cannot count on external systems to support you, you must create your own systems. When hospitals would not treat you, when funeral homes would not serve you, when social services did not care about your community, you learned to care for each other.

Even when resources were scarce. When there was not enough money for proper funerals, communities pooled resources. When there was not enough time because everyone was working, people made time anyway. When there was not enough space in small homes, space was created. Scarcity did not prevent care. It shaped how care was offered, but it did not stop it.

And pain was abundant. So much loss. Deaths from preventable illness because healthcare was inaccessible. Deaths from violence, from lynching, from police brutality. Deaths from the grinding poverty and stress that shortened lives. Early deaths, unexpected deaths, deaths that should never have happened. And yet, communities developed ways to hold all this loss, to grieve together, to keep going.

We learned to care for one another when systems failed us. This learning was not theoretical. It was practical, immediate, essential. You learned to care for your neighbors because that was how you all survived. You learned to show up at funerals, to bring food, to sit with the grieving, because you knew that when loss came to your door, others would do the same for you.

This mutual care created bonds. It built community in the truest sense. Not just people living near each other but people caring for each other, invested in each other's wellbeing, committed to collective survival. These bonds became a source of strength, a buffer against the harms of racism and oppression, a reminder that you were not alone.

We created rituals that honored loss and celebrated life at the same time. The homegoing service that mourns death but celebrates eternal life. The repast that gathers people to grieve together but also to eat and laugh and tell stories. The practices of keeping photos of the deceased displayed, of speaking their names, of including them in family gatherings even in their absence.

These rituals hold complexity. They make space for both pain and joy, for both crying and singing, for both the reality of loss and the affirmation of ongoing connection. They do not require us to choose between grief and celebration. They allow us to hold both.

Yet even within community, grief can feel lonely. We may hesitate to burden others with our pain. We may fear being seen as weak. But healing grows when we allow ourselves to be supported, not just supportive.

Community care is powerful, but it is not without complications. Even in spaces where care is offered, receiving it can be difficult. We have been taught to be strong, to be the ones who support rather than the ones who need support. We have learned that showing vulnerability can be dangerous, that asking for help can be seen as weakness.

We may hesitate to burden others with our pain. Others are dealing with their own struggles. They have their own losses, their own stresses, their own survival to manage. We do not want to add to their load. We tell ourselves that we can handle it, that we do not need to talk about it, that others have it worse.

This hesitation is understandable but costly. It prevents us from receiving the care that community wants to offer. It isolates us even in the midst of people who care about us. It maintains the facade of strength at the expense of genuine connection and support.

We may fear being seen as weak. Weakness is not acceptable in contexts where you must be strong to survive. Where showing vulnerability can be exploited. Where falling apart is a luxury you cannot afford. So we hold ourselves together even when we are breaking. We perform strength even when we are exhausted. We hide our pain even from people who love us.

But this fear, while understandable, keeps us from the healing that comes through being truly seen. Being seen not just in our strength but also in our struggle. Not just in our capacity to endure but also in our need for support. Being seen in our wholeness, which includes both our resilience and our vulnerability.

Healing grows when we allow ourselves to be supported, not just supportive. This requires a shift. From seeing ourselves as the strong one, the helper, the rock, to recognizing that we also need help, that we also deserve care, that receiving support is not weakness but wisdom.

It requires trusting that community can hold us. That people who have supported us in the past can be supported by us now. That the care flows both ways, that sometimes we give and sometimes we receive, and that both are essential to the health of the community.

It requires practicing vulnerability. Starting small, perhaps, with one trusted person. Saying "I am struggling" instead of "I am fine." Accepting the meal that is offered instead of insisting you do not need it. Letting someone sit with you instead of assuring them you are okay. Each small act of receiving support builds capacity for more.

Community does not erase grief.
It carries it.

This distinction is important. Community care is not a cure for grief. It does not make the pain disappear. It does not bring back what was lost. It does not speed up the process of healing or shortcut the hard work of mourning.

What it does is make grief bearable. By distributing the weight across many shoulders instead of one. By providing the kind of support that allows people to feel their grief without being destroyed by it. By offering presence, witness, care, and practical help that meet immediate needs so that people have space to grieve.

Community carries grief by showing up. By bringing food so people do not have to think about cooking. By handling logistics so the bereaved do not have to manage everything alone. By staying present even when the initial shock has worn off and most people have moved on. By checking in weeks and months later, remembering that grief does not follow the calendar that society expects.

Community carries grief by creating space for it. By allowing people to cry, to be angry, to be silent, to fall apart without judgment. By not rushing people toward healing or insisting they move on. By recognizing that grief is a process that cannot be hurried, that it will take as long as it takes, and that the role of community is to be present throughout.

Community carries grief by remembering. By continuing to speak the name of the person who died. By marking anniversaries and birthdays. By keeping their memory alive through stories and rituals. By ensuring that the person is not forgotten, that their life mattered, that their loss leaves a permanent mark on the community.

Community carries grief by modeling that it is survivable. By being made up of people who have themselves experienced loss and come through it. Not unchanged, not unscathed, but alive, still capable of joy, still engaged in life. This modeling provides hope. It shows that grief does not have to be the end of everything, that life can continue even with the pain.

But community cannot carry grief if we do not let it. If we insist on carrying everything alone. If we refuse offers of help. If we hide our pain and pretend we are fine. Community can only carry what we allow it to carry, which means we must practice the vulnerability of letting others in; of showing them where we are hurting; of accepting the support they want to give.

This is the dance of communal healing. The offering and the receiving. The supporting and the being supported. The holding space for others and allowing space to be held for us. The recognition that we are all interconnected, that your grief affects me and mine affects you, that we are in this together.

In Black communities, we have always known this. We have always understood that individual and collective are intertwined. That when one of us hurts, we all hurt. That our survival depends on caring for each other. That community is not optional, it is essential.

This knowledge is part of our inheritance. It comes from ancestors who had to rely on each other to survive. Who created networks of mutual aid because that was the only way to make it through. Who understood that their wellbeing was tied to their neighbor's wellbeing. Who built community not as an abstract concept but as a daily practice of care.

We carry this forward. In how we show up for each other. In how we create space for grief and joy to coexist. In how we refuse to let anyone mourn alone. In how we keep practicing communal care even when dominant culture tells us to be individualistic, even when systems fail us, even when it would be easier to turn inward.

Because we know something that those systems do not know. That healing happens in relationship. That we need each other. That community is not just nice to have; it is necessary for survival. That grief carried together is lighter than grief carried alone.

This is our strength. Not that we do not feel pain, but that we have learned to hold pain together. Not that we do not break, but that when we do, we have people to help us gather the pieces. Not that we do not grieve, but that we grieve in community, surrounded by people who know how to sit with sorrow and still make room for life.

Community does not erase grief. It carries it. And in that carrying, it makes survival possible. It makes healing imaginable. It reminds us that we are not alone.

This is the power of holding space in Black communities. The power that has sustained us through centuries of loss. The power that continues to sustain us now. The power that we must protect, practice, and pass on to the next generation.

Because this is how we survive. Together.

Chapter 11:

Culturally Responsive Grief Care

Healing cannot be separated from identity. Who we are, where we come from, and what we believe all shape how we experience loss. When care ignores culture, it risks missing the heart of the pain.

We do not grieve in a vacuum. We grieve as ourselves, as people with particular identities, histories, values, and worldviews. Our culture shapes what we believe about death and loss, how we express emotion, what rituals we practice, what support we seek, what healing looks like.

Identity is not an add-on to grief. It is fundamental to it. A Black woman grieving the loss of her mother is not just a grieving daughter. She is a Black woman grieving in a body that carries historical trauma, in a culture with particular traditions around death and mourning, in a society that has specific expectations of her strength, in a context where her loss may be compounded by systemic factors like healthcare disparities.

To treat her grief as generic, as if her Blackness and her womanhood do not matter, is to miss essential aspects of her experience. To offer her care that was designed without Black women in mind is to provide inadequate care, care that may help superficially but fails to address the deeper layers of her pain.

Who we are shapes what we lose and how we lose it. A queer Black person grieving the loss of chosen family experiences is something different from someone grieving biological family in a context where those relationships are socially recognized and validated. An immigrant grieving someone who died in their country of origin faces complications around distance, travel, ritual participation that someone grieving locally does not.

Where we come from influences our grief. The cultural beliefs about death we absorbed growing up. The religious or spiritual frameworks we learned. The ways our families and communities modeled grief. These are not universal. They vary across cultures, across geographies, across communities. And they all shape how we understand and navigate loss.

What we believe matters profoundly. Beliefs about what happens after death, about the ongoing presence or absence of those who have died, about the meaning of suffering, about divine will or random chance, all affect how we make sense of loss. These beliefs provide comfort or create additional pain. They shape what questions we ask and what answers we can accept.

When care ignores culture, it risks missing the heart of the pain. Generic approaches to grief may address surface symptoms while missing the deeper wounds. They may offer tools that do not fit the hands that need to use them. They may provide support that feels foreign, uncomfortable, or even harmful because it does not align with the person's cultural context.

Ignoring culture is not neutrality. It is centering one particular culture, usually the dominant one, and treating it as universal. It is assuming that what works for white, middle-class, Western individuals will work for everyone. This assumption causes harm by invalidating the experiences and needs of people from other cultural backgrounds.

Missing the heart of the pain means failing to see what truly hurts. For a Black person, the heart of the pain around a death may not be just the loss itself but also the way that loss connects to larger patterns of premature death in the community, to historical losses that were never properly mourned, to the ongoing vulnerability of Black life. Care that does not account for this context cannot reach the heart of what needs healing.

Culturally responsive grief care begins with humility. It requires listening without assumptions and learning without defensiveness. It means recognizing that there is no single way to grieve and no universal timeline for healing.

Humility is the foundation. It is the recognition that as a caregiver, you do not know everything. That your training, however extensive, has limitations. That your own cultural background shapes your understanding in ways you may not fully recognize. That you have biases, blind spots, areas where you need to learn.

Humility means approaching each person as a teacher who can educate you about their experience. It means asking questions rather than making assumptions. It means being comfortable with not knowing, with sitting in uncertainty, with admitting when you are out of your depth.

This humility is particularly important when there is cultural difference between caregiver and client. A white therapist working with a Black client must approach with humility, recognizing that there are aspects of the client's experience that they may not fully understand, that their training may not have prepared them for, that they will need to learn from the client.

But humility alone is not enough. It must be paired with competence. Caregivers have a responsibility to educate themselves, to seek out training in cultural competence, to learn about the populations they serve. Clients should not bear the full burden of educating their caregivers.

It requires listening without assumptions. Listening deeply, openly, without filtering what you hear through your own cultural lens. Without assuming that you know what someone means or how they feel. Without jumping to interpretations based on your framework rather than theirs.

Listening without assumptions means catching yourself when you start to think "I know what this is about" or "this is just like..." It means staying curious even when you think you understand. It means checking your interpretations with the person rather than assuming they are accurate.

It means paying attention not just to words but to what is underneath the words. To the cultural meanings embedded in how someone describes their experience. To the values that shape what they emphasize or minimize. To the ways their identity influences what feels safe to share and what must be protected.

And learning without defensiveness. When someone tells you that something you said or did was hurtful, when they point out a bias, you were not aware of, when they challenge your assumptions, defensiveness is a natural reaction. But it is not a helpful one.

Learning requires being willing to hear feedback, to acknowledge mistakes, to change behavior. It requires managing your own discomfort so that it does not become the client's problem. It requires understanding that being called out on cultural insensitivity is not an attack on your character but an opportunity to grow.

Defensiveness shuts down learning. It centers the caregiver's feelings over the client's experience. It prevents the kind of honest communication necessary for effective care. Culturally responsive care requires the ability to receive feedback with grace, to apologize when you cause harm, and to commit to doing better.

It means recognizing that there is no single way to grieve and no universal timeline for healing. Dominant grief models often present grief as following stages or patterns. But these models are cultural constructs, developed based on populations, reflecting particular values about emotion and healing.

In reality, grief is diverse. People grieve in countless ways. Some cry openly, others grieve privately. Some need to talk, others process through silence. Some return to routines quickly, others need extended time before they can function. Some integrate their loss and move forward; others carry it forever in ways that shape but do not destroy them.

Cultural background influences all these variations. Cultures differ in how emotion should be expressed, whether grief should be public or private, how long mourning should last, what rituals should be observed, what support should be sought. Recognizing this diversity means not imposing one cultural model on everyone.

And there is no universal timeline. The idea that grief should resolve in a year, or that certain milestones should be reached by certain times, is culturally specific. In some cultures, mourning periods are prescribed and extended. In others, grief is understood as a lifelong process. Imposing external timelines on people's grief is harmful. It pressures them to move faster than they are ready, invalidates ongoing pain, suggests that they are grieving incorrectly.

Culturally responsive care respects each person's timeline. It recognizes that healing is not linear, that grief can resurface years later, that anniversaries and triggers can bring pain flooding back, that there is no endpoint where grief is fully resolved. It makes space for people to grieve at their own pace, in their own way, according to their own cultural understanding of what healing looks like.

For Black clients, culturally responsive care honors history, faith, family, and community. It understands that resilience is not the absence of pain, but the courage to survive it. It makes room for both strength and sorrow.

Honoring history means acknowledging the context of historical trauma. Recognizing that current grief is often connected to past losses, both personal and collective. Understanding that Black grief carries weight beyond the immediate loss, that it is shaped by centuries of violence, displacement, family separation, premature death.

It means not treating each loss as isolated but understanding how it fits into larger patterns. How the death of a young Black man from police violence connects to a long history of state violence against Black bodies. How the death of a Black woman from preventable illness connects to ongoing healthcare disparities and medical racism. How any loss in a Black family activates the cumulative grief of all that has been lost.

Honoring history also means recognizing resilience that has been developed over generations. The survival strategies, the cultural practices, the spiritual resources that Black communities have cultivated. Not romanticizing this resilience or using it to minimize pain but acknowledging it as real and important.

Honoring faith means understanding the central role that spirituality and religion play for many Black people. Not assuming that everyone is Christian, but recognizing that for those who are, faith is often integral to how they make sense of loss and find comfort. That scripture, prayer, church community, belief in an afterlife and reunion with loved ones, are not just peripheral but central to healing.

It means making space for spiritual language and practices in therapeutic settings. Not requiring people to translate their spiritual experiences into secular psychological terms. Not pathologizing faith or seeing it as avoidance. Understanding that for many Black people, God is who they turn to first in times of crisis, and that this turning is adaptive and healthy.

It also means recognizing when faith creates complications. When religious teachings about strength or suffering make it harder to acknowledge pain. When church communities fail to provide adequate support. When people feel abandoned by God in their grief. Honoring faith includes holding space for religious struggle, for questions and doubts, for the complex relationship many people have with their spirituality.

Honoring family means understanding that family structures and dynamics in Black communities may differ from dominant culture norms. That extended family, chosen family, and community members who function as family are all important. That decision-making may be collective rather than individual. That family loyalty and obligation are strong values.

It means not imposing individualistic frameworks on people from collectivist cultures. Not assuming that independence is always the goal or that enmeshment is always pathological. Understanding that what looks like dependence to someone from an individualistic background may be healthy interdependence in a collectivist framework.

It also means understanding how family can be both source of support and source of stress. How family expectations around strength can make it hard to be vulnerable. How family silence around certain topics can prevent healing. Honoring family does not mean idealizing it but understanding its central importance while also recognizing its complexities.

Honoring community means recognizing that healing happens in relationship, that community care is essential, that isolation is harmful. It means incorporating community into treatment when appropriate, understanding that therapy is not the only or always the primary source of support, respecting the wisdom and practices of community-based healing.

It means understanding cultural practices like homegoings, repasts, ongoing memorial events. Not seeing these as indulgent or as preventing people from moving on, but as important rituals that serve real functions in the grieving process. Supporting people's participation in these communal practices rather than suggesting they skip them.

It understands that resilience is not the absence of pain, but the courage to survive it. This reframe is crucial. Too often, Black resilience is understood as superhuman strength, as the ability to endure without breaking, as not feeling pain in the first place. This understanding is harmful. It sets impossible standards. It denies the reality of pain. It suggests that if you are struggling, you lack resilience.

True resilience is continuing despite pain, not avoiding it. It is the courage to face another day when you do not know how you will make it through. It is the ability to hold both grief and hope, both sorrow and joy, both the wound and the healing. It means to keep going while also acknowledging how hard it is to keep going.

Culturally responsive care recognizes this distinction. It does not praise people for their strength in ways that deny their pain. It does not use resilience as a reason to withhold support. It understands that being resilient does not mean you do not need help, that surviving does not mean you are not suffering, that strength and struggle coexist.

It makes room for both strength and sorrow. These are not opposites. They are not mutually exclusive. People can be strong and also be deeply sad. They can be coping and also be in pain. They can be surviving and also be barely holding on.

Culturally responsive care holds this complexity. It does not require people to choose between being strong or being vulnerable. It allows them to be both. It creates space for the full range of human emotion and experience. It supports people in their strength while also honoring their sorrow.

This means not rushing people out of their grief with reminders of their strength. Not using their past resilience to suggest they should be fine now. Not minimizing their current pain by pointing to what they have survived before. Strength and sorrow can coexist, and healing requires making space for both.

Healing grows when people feel seen.
Care becomes transformative when culture is respected.

Being seen means being recognized in your full humanity. Not just as a set of symptoms or a diagnostic category or a problem to be solved, but as a whole person with a particular identity, history, context, and set of needs. Being seen means that your cultural background is acknowledged and honored, that your experiences are validated, that your way of being in the world is respected.

When people feel seen, they can relax. They do not have to work so hard to explain themselves, to translate their experiences, to defend their reality. They can use their energy for actual healing rather than for managing the therapeutic relationship. They can be vulnerable in ways they could not be if they did not feel seen and understood.

Being seen also means being seen in your particularity. Not as a representative of your race or culture, not as a stereotype, but as an individual with your own unique combination of identities and experiences. Culturally responsive care sees the forest and the trees, understanding both cultural patterns and individual variation.

Healing grows when people feel seen because being seen is itself healing. It communicates worth. It says you matter. Your experience matters. Your pain is real and legitimate. You are not alone. These messages are profoundly therapeutic. They counter the isolation of grief, the shame of struggling, the fear that something is wrong with you.

Care becomes transformative when culture is respected. Not just acknowledged or tolerated, but actively respected. When cultural practices are incorporated into treatment. When cultural values shape goals and interventions. When cultural identity is seen as a strength and resource rather than a complication.

Respect means taking culture seriously. Not seeing it as quaint or exotic or optional. Not reducing it to surface-level elements like food and holidays. But understanding it as a deep structure that shapes worldview, values, relationships, and ways of being.

Transformative care changes people; not by forcing them to fit into predetermined models, but by providing support that is so well-matched to who they are that it reaches them. That it meets them where they are. That it works with their existing strengths and resources. That it honors their way of being while also offering new tools and perspectives.

When culture is respected, people can bring their whole selves to the healing process. They do not have to compartmentalize, leaving parts of themselves outside the therapy room or the support group or the healing space. They can integrate their cultural identity with their grief work, their spiritual beliefs with their emotional processing, their community values with their personal healing.

This integration is powerful. It allows for healing that is authentic, that feels true to who the person is, that builds on rather than fights against their cultural foundation. It creates change that is sustainable because it is congruent with the person's core identity and values.

Culturally responsive care is not perfect. Caregivers will make mistakes, miss things, inadvertently cause harm. But what makes it culturally responsive is the commitment to keep learning, to repair when harm is done, to center the needs and experiences of the people being served.

It is the difference between care that says, "fit yourself to our model" and care that says, "we will adapt our approach to fit you." Between care that ignores difference and care that celebrates it. Between care that sees culture as a barrier and care that sees it as a resource.

For Black clients seeking grief support, culturally responsive care can mean the difference between help that helps and help that harms. Between feeling seen and feeling misunderstood. Between healing and continued wounding.

This is what we deserve. Care that recognizes who we are. Care that honors where we come from. Care that respects what we believe. Care that makes space for our full humanity.

Healing cannot be separated from identity. And care that tries to separate them cannot truly heal. But care that honors the connection, that sees grief as culturally embedded, that works with rather than against cultural identity, can create profound transformation.

This is the promise of culturally responsive grief care. Not that it will take away the pain, but that it will honor the pain and the person experiencing it. Not that it will provide easy answers, but that it will hold the questions with respect. Not that it will fix everything, but that it will create space for real healing to occur.

When we are seen, when our culture is respected, when our full identity is honored, healing becomes possible in ways it could not be otherwise. This is what culturally responsive care offers. This is what all grieving people deserve. This is what we must continue to build, to practice, to demand.

CHAPTER 12:

FAITH AS RESISTANCE

Faith has always been more than belief for us; it has been resistance. It has sustained us through unimaginable loss and reminded us that we are worthy of more than survival.

In the context of Black life in America, faith has never been a luxury or a private matter. It has been essential. It has been the thing that kept people going when logic said there was no reason to hope. When the present was unbearable and the future looked bleak, faith provided an anchor. A belief that this world's cruelty was not the final word, that there was something beyond the suffering, that we were beloved even when the world treated us as disposable.

This faith sustained our ancestors through the Middle Passage. Through slavery. Through reconstruction and its violent backlash. Through Jim Crow and lynching. Through ongoing discrimination and violence. At every turn, when systems sought to break us, faith was the thing that could not be taken away. The interior life, the spiritual connection, the belief in divine justice and ultimate redemption, these remained even when everything else was stripped away.

Faith has been resistance because it has refused to accept the world's definition of our worth. When society said we were less than human, faith said we were children of God. When the world said we deserved suffering, faith said we deserved dignity. When circumstances said we should despair, faith said we should hope. This refusal to internalize our oppression, this insistence on our inherent value, this claiming of hope in the face of horror, all of this is resistance.

Faith reminded us that we are worthy of more than survival. Survival is necessary, but it is not sufficient. We are worthy not just of making it through, but of thriving. Not just of enduring, but of flourishing. Not just of existing, but of living fully. Faith holds this vision, this belief that we deserve joy, peace, freedom, wholeness. That our lives have meaning beyond the suffering imposed on us.

This faith has been deeply communal. Churches became more than houses of worship. They became centers of community life, places of political organizing, sources of mutual aid, schools and social services. The Black church has been central to every major movement for liberation, from abolition to civil rights to contemporary activism. Faith and resistance have been intertwined, each strengthening the other.

But faith must also evolve. It must move from endurance to empowerment. From silence to truth. From simply getting through to truly healing.

The faith that sustained survival is holy and necessary. But it is not always sufficient for healing. Sometimes the very faith practices that helped people endure have also kept them silent about their pain. The emphasis on strength can become a barrier to vulnerability. The focus on the afterlife can prevent us from addressing present suffering. The call to forgive can be weaponized against those seeking accountability and justice.

Moving from endurance to empowerment means claiming faith not just as something that helps us survive oppression but as something that fuels our resistance to it. Not just as consolation for suffering but as motivation to end suffering. Not just as individual comfort but as collective power.

Empowerment through faith looks like recognizing that we are made in the divine image and therefore our lives, our bodies, our wellbeing matter. That caring for ourselves and our communities is sacred work. That demanding justice is not contrary to faith but an expression of it. That God does not require our suffering, that we are allowed to want better, to fight for better, to expect better.

Moving from silence to truth means allowing faith to hold our full reality. Not just the testimony of triumph but also the lament of ongoing struggle. Not just praise but also questions. Not just certainty but also doubt. Truth-telling faith makes space for the full range of human experience, including anger at injustice, confusion about suffering, and grief over loss.

This kind of faith does not require us to spiritualize everything, to find silver linings, to rush toward resolution. It allows us to sit in the hard places, to name what hurts, to acknowledge what is wrong without immediately jumping to "but God." It trusts that God is big enough to handle our honesty, that faith is strong enough to hold our pain.

Moving from simply getting through to truly healing means recognizing that survival is not the same as healing. That functioning is not the same as thriving. That making it through another day is necessary but not sufficient. Healing requires more than endurance. It requires attention to wounds, processing of trauma, tending of grief, rebuilding of what was broken.

Faith that supports healing makes room for this deeper work. It does not equate healing with instant deliverance or pretend that prayer alone fixes everything. It recognizes that healing is a process, often a long one, that requires multiple resources including but not limited to faith. It affirms the value of therapy, of medication when needed, of community support, of rest, of professional help.

When faith affirms our right to rest, to grieve, to seek help, it becomes a tool for liberation. It reminds us that healing is not a betrayal of strength, but an expression of it.

Rest is a radical act in a culture that demands constant productivity. For Black people especially, rest has been denied, seen as laziness, punished. The legacy of slavery, where Black bodies were property to be worked to exhaustion and beyond, still shapes how rest is viewed. To claim the right to rest is to reject that legacy, to assert that our worth is not determined by our output, that we are human beings deserving of recuperation and renewal.

When faith affirms our right to rest, when it reclaims rest as holy rather than shameful, it liberates us from the tyranny of endless striving. It gives us permission to stop, to breathe, to sleep, to cease from labor. It reminds us of Sabbath, of the divine modeling of rest, of rest as essential to creation and re-creation.

Grieving is also radical. In a culture that wants us to move on quickly, to be productive even in our pain, to not disrupt things with our sorrow, choosing to grieve, to take time with our grief, to honor it rather than suppress it, is resistance. And when faith affirms this right, when it makes space for lament alongside praise, when it recognizes grief as a necessary response to loss rather than a failure of faith, it supports our healing.

Seeking help challenges the narrative of superhuman Black strength. It says we are human, we have limits, we need support. When faith affirms this, when it recognizes that asking for help is wisdom not weakness, when it sees therapy and medication and professional support as tools God can work through rather than evidence of insufficient faith, it frees people to access the care they need.

All of this is liberation. Liberation from narratives that harm us. Liberation from expectations that exhaust us. Liberation from silence that isolates us. Faith that affirms rest, grief, and help-seeking is faith that wants us free, not just surviving but thriving, not just enduring but healing.

It reminds us that healing is not a betrayal of strength, but an expression of it. The belief that seeking healing means you are weak is a lie. Healing requires immense strength. It takes courage to face your pain rather than avoid it. It takes strength to be vulnerable, to ask for help, to do the hard work of recovery. It takes power to choose healing when everything in you wants to shut down.

True strength includes knowing when you need support and having the courage to seek it. It includes being honest about your struggles rather than performing fine-ness. It includes taking care of yourself so that you can continue to show up for what matters. This is not weakness disguised as strength. This is actual strength, the kind that sustains over the long term rather than burning out.

I remember the day like yesterday. Weeks after my dad died. I was twenty-eight years old, and I had been trying so hard to pray my way through. Trying to affirm my way through. Repeating scriptures. Claiming promises. Asking God to take the pain away, to give me strength, to help me keep going.

But nothing was working.

I was sinking, fast. The grief was pulling me under, and no amount of prayer seemed to stop it. I would wake up and immediately feel the weight pressing down on my chest. I would try to read my Bible and the words would blur. I would attempt to pray, and the prayers would die in my throat, replaced by silent screams that I could not release.

I had been taught that faith was enough. That if I just believed hard enough, prayed long enough, trusted deeply enough, God would deliver me. That this grief, like all suffering, was something to be endured with quiet strength and unshakable faith. That asking for help outside of prayer meant my faith was insufficient.

But I was drowning. And faith alone, as I had been practicing it, was not keeping me afloat.

I was in the living room when it happened. My sister was there. My brother-in-law was there. And I looked up at them, these people who loved me and knew me, and I spoke the words that I had been afraid to speak. The words that felt like admission of failure, like proof that I was not strong enough, not faithful enough.

"I need help."
Three words. Simple. Terrifying. Honest.
I need help.

Not "I'll be fine." Not "I'm trusting God." Not "prayer is getting me through." But the raw, vulnerable truth. I need help. I cannot do this alone. What I am doing is not working. I am not okay.

My brother-in-law heard me. Really heard me. He did not tell me to pray harder. He did not question my faith. He did not suggest that seeking help meant I did not trust God. He simply acted.

He immediately connected me with a therapist. Made the call. Set up the appointment. Removed the barriers between me and the help I needed. And in that moment, his response was grace. It was faith in action. It was the embodiment of the kind of support that does not spiritualize suffering but addresses it practically, compassionately, urgently.

That therapist became the beginning of my healing journey. Not the end of it, because healing is not a destination but a process. But the beginning. The place where I could finally say out loud all the things I had been holding inside. Where I could cry without judgment. Where I could express anger without being told to forgive faster. Where I could sit with my pain without rushing toward resolution.

Therapy did not replace my faith. It complemented it. It gave me tools that prayer alone had not provided. It created space for processing that church had not offered. It allowed me to be human in my grief, to feel the full weight of what I had lost without spiritualizing it away.

And slowly, very slowly, I began to surface. Not because therapy fixed me or because I finally prayed the right prayer. But because I had stopped trying to do it alone. Because I had allowed myself to be vulnerable. Because I had spoken the words "I need help" and been met with support instead of judgment.

That moment in the living room, that confession of need, that reaching out for help, that was not a failure of faith. It was faith evolving. It was faith big enough to acknowledge human limitation. It was faith that trusted God could work through therapists and professional support, not just through prayer and Scripture alone.

It was the moment I learned that asking for help is not weakness. It is wisdom. It is recognizing that we are not meant to carry everything alone, that healing often requires more than we can provide for ourselves, that there is no shame in needing support.

Faith does not ask us to hide our wounds.
It invites us to bring them into the light.

The faith that asks us to hide our wounds, to pretend we are not hurting, to smile through pain, to testify before we have healed, is not liberating faith. It is faith that has been shaped by respectability politics, by the need to present well to the white gaze, by the belief that showing vulnerability gives ammunition to those who want to harm us.

But liberating faith, faith rooted in the full witness of Scripture, faith that remembers Job's complaints and Jeremiah's weeping and Jesus' anguish, knows that wounds need light to heal. That what we hide festers. That bringing our wounds into the light, showing them to God and to trusted community, is the beginning of healing.

This invitation to bring wounds into the light is an invitation to honesty. To stop performing. To bring our whole selves, wounded and struggling and imperfect, into relationship with the divine and with each other. It is an invitation to trust that we will be met with compassion rather than judgment, with care rather than condemnation.

When we bring our wounds into the light, we discover we are not alone. Others have wounds too. Others are struggling too. The light reveals not just our individual pain but our collective vulnerability, and in that revelation, connection becomes possible. Isolation gives way to community. Shame gives way to shared humanity.

Faith as resistance means resisting the forces that want us silent, that want us performing strength we do not feel, that want us hiding pain that needs attention. It means claiming our right to be fully human, fully complex, fully honest about our experiences. It means using faith not as a mask to hide behind but as a foundation to stand on while we do the vulnerable work of healing.

This is the faith we need. Not faith that demands we suppress ourselves, but faith that empowers us to be ourselves. Not faith that adds to our burdens, but faith that helps us carry them. Not faith that keeps us silent, but faith that gives us voice.

Faith as resistance. Faith as healing. Faith as liberation. This is our inheritance. This is our right. This is what we claim.

CHAPTER 13:

MY CALLING TO SOCIAL WORK

Grief did not only break me open, it redirected my life. What once felt like an ending slowly became an invitation. An invitation to look at pain differently. To sit with others in their sorrow. To help create spaces where healing feels possible.

The losses that shattered my world also showed me a path forward. In the depths of grief, when I was searching for support and finding gaps, when I was trying to understand why the help available did not fit my needs, when I was feeling profoundly alone in my pain, seeds were being planted. I did not recognize them then. I was too focused on survival. But looking back, I can see how those experiences of isolation and inadequacy shaped what would become my life's work.

What once felt like an ending, the death of the person I was, the death of the future I had imagined, the death of my sense of how the world worked, slowly became an invitation. Not immediately. Not all at once. But gradually, as I moved through my grief, as I began to heal in small increments, I started to notice what was missing. I started to wonder why resources for Black grievers were so scarce. I started to imagine what better support might look like.

An invitation to look at pain differently. Not as something to be avoided or quickly resolved, but as something that carries information. Something that reveals gaps in our systems and opportunities for change. Something that, when witnessed and honored, can become a doorway to deeper understanding and connection.

To sit with others in their sorrow. This became a calling. To offer the presence I had needed but not always found. To create the kind of space where people could bring their full grief without judgment or pressure to move on. To simply be with people in their pain, not trying to fix it but witnessing it, honoring it, holding space for it.

To help create spaces where healing feels possible. Where people are seen in their cultural context. Where their experiences are validated. Where they are not alone. Where resources are available and accessible. Where the support offered matches the needs present. Where healing is understood as a process, not a destination. Where both individual and collective dimensions of grief are addressed.

I did not come to social work because I wanted a career. I came because I needed language for what I had lived. I needed to understand the systems that shaped my grief, the gaps that left me feeling unseen, and the power of connection when everything feels lost.

My entry into social work was personal before it was professional. It was driven by my own experience of navigating grief without adequate support. By my encounters with therapists who did not understand. By my search for resources that reflected my reality. By my need to make sense of what had happened to me and why the healing process had been so difficult.

I needed language for what I had lived. The words to describe somatic grief, historical trauma, cultural bereavement, ambiguous loss. The frameworks to understand how racism affects mental health, how trauma is passed through generations, how resilience and vulnerability coexist. The concepts that helped me see that what I experienced was not personal failure but normal response to abnormal circumstances.

I needed to understand the systems that shaped my grief. Why research excluded Black experiences. Why therapy felt unsafe. Why mental health services were not accessible or culturally responsive. How structural racism creates health disparities. How poverty and discrimination compound grief. How systems fail the very people who need them most. Understanding these systems helped me see that my struggle was not just personal, it was also political.

The gaps that left me feeling unseen became clearer as I learned more. The absence of Black representation in grief research and literature. The lack of culturally competent clinicians. The scarcity of resources addressing the specific ways Black communities grieve. The silence around certain kinds of losses. These gaps were not accidental. They were the result of systemic exclusion, of Black experiences being marginalized, of dominant narratives being treated as universal.

And the power of connection when everything feels lost became something I wanted to facilitate for others. Because I knew firsthand how isolating grief could be. How much difference it made when someone truly understood. How healing it was to share my story and have it witnessed. How community care had sustained me when formal systems failed. I wanted to create more of that connection, to build bridges between isolated grievers, to foster the kind of community care that had helped me survive.

My education gave me tools, but my grief gave me purpose. It taught me that empathy is not theoretical, it is embodied. That listening is not passive; it is an act of care. And that healing is never just individual, it is collective.

The social work education was valuable. It provided frameworks, skills, knowledge, ethical guidelines. It taught me about assessment, intervention, documentation, systems thinking. It exposed me to theories and research. It offered supervised practice experiences. All of this was important and necessary.

But my grief gave me purpose. It gave me the why behind the what. It connected my learning to lived experience in ways that made the work meaningful. It ensured that my path forward would be grounded not just in theory but in the real needs of real people who were suffering. It kept me focused on what helps versus what is supposed to help.

It taught me that empathy is not theoretical, it is embodied. You cannot truly empathize with grief from a purely intellectual place. You have to know it in your body, in your heart, in your life. This knowing, this embodied understanding, transforms how you sit with others in their pain. You are not an observer analyzing from a distance but a fellow human who has walked similar terrain.

That listening is not passive; it is an act of care. Listening deeply, fully, without agenda or judgment, is profoundly active. It requires presence, attention, the setting aside of your own thoughts and reactions. It requires creating space for another person's truth. It requires believing what you hear. This kind of listening is care made manifest. It says you matter. Your experience matters. I am here with you.

And that healing is never just individual, it is collective. We do not heal in isolation. Our healing is connected to our communities, to those who came before us, to those who will come after. When one person heals, they create possibility for others. When we heal together, we transform not just individuals but systems, cultures, patterns that have caused harm. Collective healing addresses root causes, not just symptoms. It creates conditions for sustained wellbeing, not just temporary relief.

This calling is not about fixing people. It is about walking with them.

The savior complex has no place in healing work. The idea that I, as a professional, have all the answers and my role is to fix broken people, is harmful. It centers me instead of the person seeking help. It assumes pathology instead of recognizing resilience. It ignores the person's own wisdom and agency.

This calling is about companionship. About walking alongside people in their grief journey. Not leading them, not dragging them, not pushing them, but walking with them. At their pace. On their path. Offering support and witness and presence. Being willing to sit with the not-knowing, the messiness, the non-linear process of healing.

Walking with people means honoring their autonomy. Recognizing that they are the experts on their own lives. That my role is to support their healing, not to impose my vision of what their healing should look like. That I bring professional knowledge and skills, but they bring lived experience and self-knowledge, and both are essential.

It means being humble. Acknowledging that I do not have all the answers. That healing is mysterious and individual. That what works for one person may not work for another. That I will make mistakes and need to be willing to learn from them. That the person I am walking with has much to teach me.

It means being present. Not just physically but emotionally, spiritually, fully. Being with people in their pain without trying to escape it or make it go away. Tolerating discomfort. Sitting with uncertainty. Trusting the process even when it is slow and difficult.

This is the work I was called to. Not as a career but as a vocation. Not as a job but as a ministry in the broadest sense. A calling to serve, to accompany, to witness, to create space for healing. A calling born from my own grief, shaped by my own journey, offered in service to others who are walking similar paths.

Chapter 14:

WHAT I WANT EVERY PROVIDER TO KNOW

Grief does not look the same in everybody. It does not follow a schedule. It does not respond to formulas. And it does not separate itself from culture, faith, or history.

This is the foundation. If providers understand nothing else, they must understand this. Grief is diverse. It is shaped by countless factors including personality, culture, relationship to the deceased, circumstances of the death, available support, previous losses, current stressors, and so much more. There is no template that works for everyone.

Grief does not look the same in everybody. Some people cry openly and often. Others grieve with dry eyes. Some withdraw and need solitude. Others seek connection constantly. Some express through words. Others through art, movement, silence. Some show physical symptoms. Others experience primarily emotional or spiritual pain. All of these are valid expressions of grief.

It does not follow a schedule. The stages of grief, however useful as a general framework, are not a checklist to be completed in order. People do not move neatly from denial to anger to bargaining to depression to acceptance. They cycle through emotions. They experience multiple feelings simultaneously. They revisit stages they thought they had moved through. They grieve in their own time, which may be much longer or different from expected timelines.

It does not respond to formulas. There is no one-size-fits-all intervention. What helps one person may not help another. Evidence-based practices are useful, but they must be applied flexibly, adapted to the individual, combined with clinical judgment and cultural competence. Healing is an art as much as a science.

And it does not separate itself from culture, faith, or history. Grief is always contextual. It is shaped by the cultural meanings people bring to death and loss, by their spiritual beliefs about what happens after death, by their family and community practices around mourning, by their historical experiences of loss and survival. Trying to treat grief as if these factors do not matter is like trying to understand a word without knowing the language it comes from.

What I want every provider to know is simple: listen first. Before offering strategies, before diagnosing, before explaining, listen. Honor the story being shared. Believe the pain being named.

Listen first. This seems obvious, but in practice, providers often jump too quickly to intervention. To offering advice, suggesting coping strategies, providing psychoeducation. All of these have their place, but not before deep listening has occurred. Not before the person has been truly heard.

Listening first means creating space for the person to tell their story. Their whole story, not just the parts that fit into intake forms. The story of who they lost, what that person meant to them, how the death occurred, what the aftermath has been like. The story of their cultural background, their family patterns around grief, their spiritual beliefs, their previous experiences with loss. The story of their current life, the other stressors they are managing, the supports they have and do not have.

Before offering strategies. Strategies are useful, but only when they are offered at the right time and in the right way. If someone has not been heard, if their experience has not been validated, they are not ready to receive strategies. They will feel like you are trying to fix them before you have understood them. Listening must come first. Understanding must precede intervention.

Before diagnosing. Not every grief response requires a diagnosis. Much of what people experience after loss is normal, even when it is painful and disruptive. Rushing to diagnose can pathologize normal grief. It can make people feel like something is wrong with them when they are responding appropriately to an abnormal situation. Listen first. Understand what they are experiencing. Then, if a diagnosis is appropriate, offer it with care and explanation.

Before explaining. Providers sometimes explain too much too soon. Explaining how grief works, what to expect, what is normal. This can be helpful, but only after you have understood this person's experience. Because if your explanation does not match their reality, it will feel invalidating. Listen to their experience before offering your knowledge. Make sure your explanations are responsive to what they have shared.

Honor the story being shared. This means treating it with reverence. Recognizing that sharing is an act of trust. Receiving it with care. Not interrupting or redirecting. Not imposing your interpretations. Not minimizing or comparing. Simply witnessing and acknowledging the story as it is offered.

Believe the pain being named. This is crucial. Believe people when they tell you how much they are hurting. Do not assume they are exaggerating. Do not compare their pain to others. Do not suggest it should not be this hard. Trust that they are the experts on their own experience. Validate their pain even if you do not fully understand it.

I learned this lesson the hard way, from both sides of the therapeutic relationship.

For many years, I had a strict rule. After being dismissed and misguided by white therapists for so long, my clinicians had to be Black women. This was not a preference. It was a requirement born from experience, from pain, from too many sessions where I had to explain things that should not have needed explaining.

My thought process behind this decision was straightforward. I could sit in a space where the Black and woman dynamics were already understood. Where I would not have to educate my therapist about microaggressions before I could talk about how they affected me. Where I would not have to justify why certain experiences were racist. Where the lived reality of navigating the world as a Black woman was simply known, felt, shared.

I thought this understanding would create the safety I needed to heal. And in some ways, it did. There was comfort in being seen by someone who got it, who knew without my having to explain, who understood the weight we carry simply by existing in these bodies in this world.

But what I found in these spaces surprised me. Because we had similar lived experiences as Black women, because we both knew what it meant to have to be strong and move along and be productive, they always tried to rush me toward healing so I could be free to do again.

Not intentionally. Not maliciously. But the same cultural conditioning that had shaped my approach to grief had shaped theirs. The same messages about strength and resilience and not staying down too long. The same pressure to function, to produce, to keep going. The same discomfort with sitting in pain for extended periods.

They wanted me to feel better. They wanted me to be free. They wanted me to reclaim my life. And in their urgency to help me get there, they moved too fast. They pushed when I needed them to sit. They offered solutions when I needed them to witness. They focused on my future when I was still trying to make sense of my past.

I cycled through several Black women therapists, each one skilled and caring, each one unable to give me what I needed. And I began to wonder if healing was possible for me at all. If maybe I was too broken, too stuck, too resistant to the very help I claimed to want.

But as fate would have it, the therapist who listened to me, who cared for me, who walked slowly alongside me, was a white presenting man.

The irony.

After years of insisting that only a Black woman could understand me, the person who finally reached me did not share my race or my gender. I almost did not give him a chance. Almost let my rule, my requirement, my very reasonable boundary prevent me from receiving the care I desperately needed.

But something made me stay. Maybe desperation. Maybe divine intervention. Maybe the recognition that he was doing something different, something the others had not done.

His approach was different in that he acknowledged that to heal the now adult late thirties version of me, we had to go back in time. We had to go back to thirteen-year-old me who got the news on a Sunday morning in 1999 that her mom died.

This seemed obvious in retrospect. Of course, my current grief was connected to my past grief. Of course, the woman I had become was shaped by the girl I had been, the losses I had experienced, the ways I had learned to survive. But no one else had made this connection so explicitly. No one else had suggested that healing adult me required attending to the wounds of adolescent me.

He understood something the others had missed. That I had never really grieved my mother. That thirteen-year-old me had been rushed through the mourning process, expected to be strong, to keep going, to not fall apart. That I had learned to perform resilience before I understood what I was performing. That decades later, that unprocessed grief was still living in my body, still shaping my responses, still waiting to be acknowledged and held.

So, we went back. Week after week, we sat with that thirteen-year-old girl. We let her cry the tears she had been told to dry. We let her express the anger she had been taught to suppress. We let her ask the questions she had been afraid to voice. We let her grieve in the way she should have been allowed to grieve then but was not.

He did not rush her. Did not rush me. He understood that healing trauma requires moving at the pace of the traumatized part, not the pace of the functional adult who has learned to cope. He knew that real transformation happens slowly, in the space between sessions, in the gradual integration of what has been split off.

The irony of finding this healing with someone who did not share my identity forced me to reckon with my own assumptions. About who could help me. About what healing required. About the complex relationship between cultural competence and individual capacity to sit with pain.

He was not perfect. There were moments when his whiteness and maleness limited his understanding, and I had to explain things. Times when I wished he knew what he could not know. But what he had, what mattered most, was the willingness to go slow. To follow rather than lead. To trust the process even when it was uncomfortable. To believe that healing was possible even when it was not visible.

And that made all the difference.

This experience taught me nuance that I carry into my work now. Cultural competence matters immensely. Representation matters. Shared identity can create safety and understanding that crosses identity lines cannot always replicate. And for many people, having a therapist who shares their background is not just preferred but necessary for healing to occur.

But cultural competence is not the only thing that matters. The ability to slow down, to truly listen, to resist the urge to fix, to sit with discomfort, to trust the client's pace, these matter too. Sometimes profoundly.

What I want every provider to know is that both things can be true. That we should absolutely strive for more Black therapists, more diversity in the field, more culturally responsive care. And that in the meantime, providers who do not share their clients' identity can still provide meaningful help if they approach with humility, if they listen deeply, if they do not rush, if they believe what they are told.

The Black women therapists who could not help me were not bad therapists. They were good therapists shaped by the same cultural forces that shaped me. What they lacked was not skill or caring but freedom from the internalized messages about productivity and strength that made sitting with long-term grief uncomfortable.

The white man who could help me was not a better therapist. He was a different therapist with different strengths and different limitations. What he had was the ability to slow down in ways that, ironically, his distance from my cultural conditioning allowed.

This is not a prescription. This is not me saying that white therapists are better or that Black therapists are too rushed or that cultural competence does not matter. This is me saying that healing is complex. That sometimes what we think we need is not what helps us. That requirements we set, however reasonable, can sometimes limit our options in ways that harm us.

When clients feel seen, healing begins. When culture is respected, trust grows. And when care is rooted in humility, transformation becomes possible.

Feeling seen is foundational to healing. When people feel that someone truly understands them, when their experience is recognized and validated, when they are not alone in their pain, healing becomes possible in ways it could not be otherwise. Being seen creates safety. And safety is necessary for the vulnerable work of grief.

When culture is respected, trust grows. For clients whose cultural background differs from the provider's, respect for culture determines whether the therapeutic relationship can develop. If they feel their culture is dismissed or pathologized, they will not trust. But when culture is actively honored, when it is seen as a resource, when culturally specific practices and beliefs are incorporated into care, trust deepens. And trust is essential for effective therapy.

And when care is rooted in humility, transformation becomes possible. Humility means the provider does not position themselves as the expert who has all the answers. It means acknowledging limitations, being willing to learn, admitting mistakes. This humility creates space for the client's own wisdom to emerge, for their agency to be honored, for real transformation rather than forced compliance.

Compassion must meet culture.
Context must guide care.

Compassion without cultural understanding is insufficient. Good intentions are not enough. Providers must combine genuine care with cultural competence. They must be willing to learn about the cultures of the people they serve, to examine their own biases, to adapt their practice to honor cultural differences.

Compassion that meets culture looks like a provider who cares deeply about their Black client and educates themselves about Black grief, about historical trauma, about the role of spirituality in Black communities. Who combines empathy with understanding, warmth with competence.

Context must guide care. Every clinical decision should be made with context in mind. The person's cultural background, their current circumstances, their available resources, their previous experiences. One-size-fits-all approaches ignore context. Effective care is contextually informed, adapted to the specific needs and situation of each person.

This is what I want every provider to know. That grief is complex and individual. That listening is primary. That cultural competence is not optional. That humility is essential. That compassion and competence must work together. That context always matters.

When providers understand these things, when they practice from this foundation, they can offer truly healing care. Care that honors the full humanity of the people they serve. Care that creates space for authentic healing. Care that makes a real difference in people's lives.

CHAPTER 15

A NEW VISION FOR GRIEF RESEARCH

We cannot heal what we refuse to study. And we cannot study what we refuse to see.

This is the challenge facing grief research. For too long, Black experiences of grief have been refused. Refused attention. Refused resources. Refused inclusion in research that claims to be universal. This refusal has consequences. It means we do not have the knowledge base to effectively support Black grievers. It means interventions are developed without Black input and then applied to Black communities as if they should work equally well. It means Black pain is invisible in the data.

We cannot heal what we refuse to study. If we do not research how racism affects grief, we cannot address it. If we do not study how historical trauma compounds current loss, we cannot heal it. If we do not investigate culturally specific grief practices, we cannot support them. The absence of research is not neutral. It is a form of neglect that harms communities by leaving their needs unaddressed.

And we cannot study what we refuse to see. Seeing requires acknowledging. Acknowledging that Black grief is different in significant ways. That it carries additional weight. That it deserves specific attention. That the gaps in current research are not accidental but the result of systemic exclusion. Refusing to see allows the status quo to continue, allows harm to persist under the guise of colorblindness.

The future of grief research must be inclusive, intersectional, and community informed. It must value lived experience as much as empirical data. It must ask new questions and challenge old assumptions.

Inclusive means including Black participants in meaningful numbers in all grief research. Not as tokens or afterthoughts, but as central to the study. Oversampling if necessary to ensure adequate representation. Recruiting from diverse Black communities to capture the full range of Black experiences. Including Black researchers on the team, not just as research assistants but as principal investigators and thought leaders.

Intersectional means recognizing that people hold multiple identities that shape their experiences. That Black grief is also shaped by gender, sexuality, class, ability, geography, and other factors. That a Black queer woman's grief may differ from a Black straight man's grief. That intersectionality must inform research design, analysis, and interpretation.

Community-informed means involving Black communities in every stage of the research process. From identifying research questions to designing studies to interpreting findings to disseminating results. Community-based participatory research models that center community needs and build community capacity. Research that serves communities, not just the careers of researchers.

It must value lived experience as much as empirical data. Quantitative data is important, but it cannot capture everything. Qualitative research that centers narratives, that allows people to describe their experiences in their own words, is equally valuable. Mixed methods approaches that combine numbers and stories provide the fullest picture. And community knowledge, the wisdom held by people who have lived these experiences, must be recognized as a legitimate form of knowledge.

It must ask new questions and challenge old assumptions. Not just applying existing frameworks to Black populations but asking what Black experiences reveal that existing frameworks miss. Challenging the assumption that grief models developed on white populations are universal. Questioning whether concepts like "complicated grief" or "prolonged grief disorder" adequately account for cultural differences and contextual factors. Developing new theories grounded in Black experiences.

When Black voices are centered, the field becomes richer. When our stories are included, care becomes more effective. Representation does not dilute science, it strengthens it.

Centering Black voices means more than including them as subjects. It means having Black researchers shape the questions, the methods, the interpretations. It means Black scholars being cited, published, funded, promoted. It means Black perspectives informing theory development, not just being added to existing theories as an afterthought.

When this happens, when Black voices are truly centered, the entire field benefits. New insights emerge. Existing theories are challenged and refined. The understanding of grief becomes more comprehensive, more nuanced, more accurate. Everyone's knowledge expands.

When our stories are included, when Black experiences of grief are researched and understood, care becomes more effective. Interventions can be developed that work for Black communities. Clinicians can be trained in approaches that are culturally responsive. Resources can be created that reflect Black realities. The gaps that currently exist begin to close.

Representation does not dilute science, it strengthens it. The fear that including diverse perspectives will somehow weaken scientific rigor is unfounded. In reality, homogeneous samples produce limited findings that cannot be generalized. Diverse samples produce more robust findings that better represent human diversity. Inclusion makes science better, not worse.

Our pain is not marginal.
Our healing is essential.

Black pain is not a niche concern. It is not marginal to the study of grief. It is central. Because Black people are a significant portion of the population. Because racism affects health outcomes in profound ways. Because understanding how oppression compounds grief is essential to understanding grief itself.

Treating Black pain as marginal allows it to be ignored. Allows research to proceed without Black inclusion. Allows theories to be developed that do not account for Black experiences. This marginalization is harmful. It perpetuates the very gaps that leave Black grievers without adequate support.

Our healing is essential. Not just for Black people, though that alone would be sufficient justification. But for everyone. Because when we understand grief more fully, when we account for cultural and contextual factors, when we develop more nuanced and flexible approaches, everyone benefits. The healing of Black communities contributes to the healing of the larger society.

This new vision for grief research is not just aspirational. It is necessary. Necessary for justice. Necessary for accuracy. Necessary for effective care. The field must change. It must become more inclusive, more humble, more responsive to the needs of all grieving people.

This change is already beginning. There are Black researchers doing groundbreaking work. There are studies being conducted that center Black experiences. There is growing recognition of the need for cultural competence in grief care. But there is still so much work to be done.

The future of grief research depends on our willingness to change course. To acknowledge past exclusions. To commit to present inclusion. To build toward future equity. When we do this, when we create research that truly represents human diversity, we create the foundation for care that can heal.

CLOSING:

WE ARE WORTH THE HEALING

This book is not a conclusion; it is an opening. An invitation to see grief not as something to hide, but as something to honor. To recognize that our stories carry wisdom, and our pain deserves care.

We have reached the end of these pages, but not the end of the journey. Grief is ongoing. Healing is ongoing. The work of creating better support for Black grievers is ongoing. This book is a beginning, a door opening onto new possibilities, new conversations, new commitments.

An invitation to see grief not as something to hide. For too long, we have been taught to conceal our pain. To grieve privately. To not burden others. To move on quickly. This book invites a different approach. To see grief as a natural, necessary, important response to loss. To give it space, honor it, allow it to be seen.

But as something to honor. Honor means treating with respect and reverence. It means recognizing grief as sacred, as carrying important information, as deserving our attention and care. When we honor grief, we honor the love that preceded it, the person who was lost, the impact their absence has created. We honor our own capacity to feel deeply, to be affected by loss, to carry pain and continue living.

To recognize that our stories carry wisdom. The stories of how we have grieved, how we have survived, how we have found ways to continue despite devastating loss. These stories are not just personal narratives. They are sources of knowledge. They teach us about resilience, about community care, about cultural practices that sustain. They carry wisdom that deserves to be shared, learned from, passed on.

And our pain deserves care. Not dismissal. Not minimization. Not rushing. But genuine care. Attention. Support. Resources. Space to unfold at its own pace. Compassion that meets us where we are. This care is not a luxury. It is a necessity. It is what we deserve simply by virtue of being human, of having experienced loss, of carrying pain.

We have carried so much for so long. It is time to set some of it down.

The burdens we carry are heavy. The grief, yes, but also the historical trauma. The ongoing discrimination. The expectation to be strong. The pressure to perform. The silencing of our pain. The lack of support. The isolation. The exhaustion. We have carried these things because we had to, because survival demanded it, because there was no alternative.

But carrying everything forever is not sustainable. It breaks us down. It costs us our health, our wellbeing, our capacity for joy. At some point, we must begin to set some of it down. Not all at once. Not completely. But gradually, intentionally, with support.

Setting it down might mean finally allowing ourselves to grieve. To stop performing strength and be honest about our pain.

To cry the tears we have been holding back. To speak the words we have been keeping inside.

It might mean seeking help. Professional support. Therapy. Community. Medical care. Whatever we need and have been denying ourselves because we thought we should be able to handle it alone.

It might mean resting. Actually resting. Not just sleeping but ceasing from constant productivity. Giving ourselves permission to stop, to be still, to recuperate.

It might mean saying no. To additional responsibilities. To others' expectations. To demands on our time and energy that we cannot meet without harming ourselves.

Setting it down is not giving up. It is choosing to live. Choosing healing over endless endurance. Choosing wholeness over fragmentation. Choosing ourselves.

We are worthy of rest.
We are worthy of compassion.
We are worthy of healing.
And we always have been.

This worthiness is not earned. It is inherent. We do not have to prove we deserve rest by working ourselves to exhaustion first. We do not have to earn compassion by being strong enough or struggling hard enough. We do not have to justify our need for healing. We are worthy simply because we are human.

We are worthy of rest. Of sleep. Of Sabbath. Of time away from labor. Of moments when we do not have to be productive or useful or serving others. We are worthy of rest that restores, that renews, that allows us to reconnect with ourselves and what matters most.

We are worthy of compassion. From others and from ourselves. Worthy of kindness when we struggle. Worthy of understanding when we cannot do it all. Worthy of grace when we make mistakes or fall short. Worthy of care that is tender and patient and attentive to our needs.

We are worthy of healing. Worthy of support and resources. Worthy of care that honors our cultural context and lived experiences. Worthy of spaces where we can be our full selves. Worthy of time and attention and commitment to our wellbeing. Worthy of the hard, slow, sacred work of healing from all we have endured.

And we always have been. This worthiness was not created by this book. It was not granted by any external authority. It has always been true. We were worthy before we knew we were worthy. Before anyone told us. Before we could claim it for ourselves. This truth has been waiting for us to recognize it, to believe it, to live from it.

We are worth the healing. Every bit of effort it takes. Every resource it requires. Every moment of time and attention. We are worth it. Our lives are worth it. Our wellbeing is worth it. Our future is worth it.

This is the message of this book. Not that grief is easy or that healing is quick or that everything will be okay. But that we matter. Our pain matters. Our healing matters. We deserve support. We deserve care. We deserve to be seen, honored, held.

And we are worthy of claiming this. Of insisting on it. Of building it for ourselves and each other. Of creating the conditions for healing that have been denied us. Of refusing to accept less than we deserve.

We are worth the healing. And the healing is possible. Not perfect. Not complete. Not without ongoing work. But real. True. Available.

This is where we begin. With this recognition. This claiming. This commitment.

We are worth the healing.
We always have been.
And now we know it